A GRIM ALMANAC OF
MANCHESTER

A Grim Almanac of
MANCHESTER

Michala Hulme

For Joan Leach and my George

First published 2015
The History Press
The Mill, Brimscombe Port
Stroud, Gloucestershire, GL5 2QG
www.thehistorypress.co.uk

Reprinted 2016

British Library Cataloguing in Publication Data.
A catalogue record for this book is available from the British Library.

ISBN 978 0 7509 6150 9

Typesetting and origination by The History Press
Printed in Great Britain

CONTENTS

ABOUT THE AUTHOR

Michala Hulme is a historian and genealogist who became interested in the history of Manchester after researching the ancestry of her family, who originated from Newton Heath.

Michala specialised in local history while undertaking a BA (Hons) Degree at Manchester Metropolitan University. Her undergraduate thesis entitled 'The Origins and Early Years of Philip's Park Cemetery' was shortlisted for Best Dissertation in Regional and Local History. She is currently working towards a PhD at MMU.

Michala has written for *Who Do You Think You Are* magazine and can be heard regularly on BBC local radio. She lives in Cheshire.

INTRODUCTION

On a dark, wet and dreary night in September 1844, a draper's assistant named Edward Mellish decided to go for a drink after work. Shortly after ten o'clock, he left a beerhouse on Oldham Street and sought the services of a prostitute named Elizabeth Kirk. Along with another prostitute named Elizabeth Lee, Kirk walked with him to Back Piccadilly, where the girls earned their wages. While Mellish was distracted, Kirk and Lee stole a sovereign out of his purse and disappeared into the night.

The same year, German philosopher Friedrich Engels passed through Manchester whilst on his tour of manufacturing districts in England. He described an area just off Oxford Road known as Little Ireland:

> The cottages are old, dirty and the smallest sort, the streets are uneven, fallen into ruts and in part without drains or pavement: masses of refuse, offal and sickening filth lie among standing pools in all directions; the atmosphere is poisoned by the effluvia from these, and laden and darkened by the smoke of a dozen tall factory chimneys. A horde of ragged women and children swarm about here, as filthy as the swine that thieve upon the garbage heaps and in the puddles ...

By the time Engels arrived in Manchester, the city had experienced change on an unprecedented scale. Between 1780 and 1800, the population had doubled. It had gone from being a relatively small market town to the industrial centre of the North. This change was brought by cotton: industrialisation made manufacturers and merchants rich, and introduced a new 'class' of men into society.

As the wealth of the mill owners and merchants increased, the workers were left to survive on low wages, in overcrowded houses filled with filth and disease. Life was grim. In Parliament Street, 380 people shared one privy. Workers lived in damp cellars with no light, no ventilation, no beds and only straw to separate them from the floor.

Hunger, poverty and desperation bred a criminal class that operated within the boundaries of the city. Lurking behind the smoke of the chimneys and the bricks of the merchant palaces was a murky underworld that would test the resolve of the governing authorities. Murderers, street gangs, thieves, fraudsters, hooligans, bigamists, drunks, prostitutes and vagabonds: all were entwined in daily life.

Sentences for criminals were harsh. Between 1552 and 1586, anyone found to be drunk was fined five shillings. Anyone unable to pay the fine was kept for six hours in the stocks. During the reign of Henry VIII, any alehouse keeper found with games on their premises such as bowls, dice or cards was fined the hefty sum of forty shillings.

In 1738, a local man named John Kilner was found guilty of selling a cow that was not marketable and fined a month's wages. Meanwhile, any woman found to be a prostitute was placed in the city's ducking stool and dumped into the pond at Daubholes (where Piccadilly is today).

In the eighteenth century, there were over 200 crimes that were punishable by death, which included horse stealing, arson, witchcraft, cutting down trees, and murder. If the criminal was lucky enough to escape the gallows, it was likely that he or she would have faced transportation for life, to a faraway country such as the Americas, and later Australia – that is if they survived being on board a hulk ship and then the long voyage to the chosen destination. Hulk ships were usually decommissioned Navy ships that had been converted into floating prisons. Life on board a hulk ship was tough and the conditions were dire: prisoners were awoken at sunrise and worked on average for ten hours a day, and were kept in chains to stop them from escaping. Overcrowding meant that the spread of disease was rife, thus leading to high mortality rates.

In 1832, serial thief John Smith was sentenced at Salford to transportation for life for stealing twenty pieces of calico. Smith – who was described as having a 'very bad' character – had already served seven years' transportation for stealing in 1825. After his conviction was announced, he was held on board the hulk ship *Cumberland*, which was moored at Chatham, until his scheduled transportation date. In March 1833, Smith was transferred to his transportation ship. He faced a journey that would last between four and six months. Not all on board would make it: tuberculosis, cholera and dysentery would claim their victims. Any inmate that misbehaved would be lashed or confined in a box in which the occupant was forced to crouch as it was so small.

Less serious criminals were often given a custodial sentence with hard labour. They were sent to one of His or Her Majesty's prisons. Manchester's current prison is HMP Manchester (although it used to be, and still is – unofficially – known as Strangeways), which was built in 1868. Alfred Waterhouse, who was the architect behind the Town Hall, designed the prison, which has a capacity to hold over 1,000 prisoners. Up until the 1960s, the prison was used to hang some of the most notorious prisoners in the country. After 1868, all executions had to be held in private; however, this did not stop crowds of people from standing outside the prison walls, shouting to their loved ones or heckling the worst offenders.

Prior to the opening of Strangeways, Manchester had two operating prisons in the nineteenth century: Belle Vue prison, which opened in 1850 and was in use until 1888 and the New Bailey prison, Salford, which opened in 1790 and closed in 1868. Before the opening of the

New Bailey prison, prisoners were held at the House of Correction, Hunt's Bank. The House of Correction could hold somewhere in the region of sixty people at any one time, although there were no toilets, fresh water or light. Prisoners often went without food.

The aim of this book is to uncover the 'grim' side of the city. It will lift the lid on the city's criminals, as well as revealing the perils of living in an industrial city – poverty, diseases, accidents, suicides and domestic abuse.

Geographically, the book tells the story of grim events that occurred in the city centre, as well as Ancoats, Ardwick, Bradford, Cheetham, Chorlton-cum-Hardy, Chorlton-on-Medlock, Collyhurst, Crumpsall, Didsbury, Gorton, Harphurhey, Hulme, Levenshulme, Longsight, Miles Platting, Moss Side, Newton Heath, Northenden, Old Trafford, Openshaw. Rusholme, Strangeways, Salford, Whalley Range and Withington.

ACKNOWLEDGEMENTS

In researching this book I would like to warmly acknowledge the help I received from Gavin Sterritt, Ayleen Hulme, Sean Hulme, Alexanda Rhys Hulme, Duncan at the Greater Manchester Police Museum, Terrance at the Victorian Picture Library, Chetham's Library, the Wellcome Library in London, Manchester Metropolitan University, Manchester Library and Archives, and anyone else that I have forgotten.

JANUARY

1 **JANUARY 1827** An elderly woman named Margaret Watson was working on her herb stall on Oldham Road when a group of drunken youths picked up some of her herbs and tossed them on the floor. Without warning, Margaret calmly reached into her apron, picked up her oyster knife and lunged at one of the youths named Dennis Meadowcroft, stabbing him in the right side of his chest and penetrating a large blood vessel. Meadowcroft immediately fell to the floor and his friends rushed to his aid. Margaret then wiped the blood off her knife with her apron and placed it back in her pocket. The young man was picked up and carried to the doctor's house, but died later.

At the inquest, Margaret Watson was found guilty of manslaughter and sent to trial. The case was heard at the Lent Assizes at Lancaster Castle. After listening to the evidence, the judge found her guilty of manslaughter and she was sentenced to six months in prison.

1907 Several newspapers reported this week on the tragic death of John William Hampson, a 50-year-old boiler fireman, who resided at Croft Street, Newton Heath.

On the day of his death, he had just finished his shift at the Heenan and Froude engineers, Newton Heath, when he was asked to stay overnight and make sure the pipes did not freeze. To do this, he had to stoke the fires every two hours. At approximately four o'clock in the morning, another worker saw Hampson lying on the floor. When he approached, he could see that Hampson was lying on top of his lamp and quite dead. His body was severely charred and his clothes were smouldering. It appeared that he may have fainted and landed on his lamp, the flames fed by his oily clothes.

2 **JANUARY 1928** A professional musician named Robert Harratt, who resided at Stockton Street, was on this day charged at the Manchester Police Court with the attempted murder of William Arthur Goodier, a lodger at the same address.

On New Year's Eve, Goodier was getting into bed when he heard a loud bang, which was followed by Mrs Harratt rushing into his room. Mrs Haratt was bleeding from the mouth and pleaded with Goodier to save her from her violent husband, at which point Goodier locked his door until Mr Harratt had gone. When the coast was clear, he crept into the next room to collect Mrs Harratt's young child. He managed to pick the child up and was nearly safe when he was met by an angry Mr Harratt, who snatched the child from his arms. Mr Harratt then reached to his hip, produced a gun, and shot Goodier. Harratt was later charged with attempted murder and remanded in custody for eight days, awaiting a trial. However, the charge of attempted murder was later dropped and the man was only prosecuted with keeping a firearm and fined £5.

3 JANUARY 1831 A shocking assassination occurred in the district of Greater Manchester. The victim was 23-year-old Thomas James Ashton, a superintendent at his father's mill.

The unfortunate event occurred after Ashton had left his father's house at seven o'clock to go to Apethorn Mill. At the same time, two mechanics – who were also taking the same route having just finished work – reported hearing gunshots and shortly after came across the lifeless body of Thomas Ashton. His body was still warm, but his face was covered with blood and froth. He had been fatally shot at close range through his heart, breaking two ribs and causing two exit wounds in his back. He had been assassinated less than 300 yards from his home.

After a lengthy police enquiry – which lasted nearly three years – James Garside and Joseph Moseley were charged with his murder. At the trial, the two men revealed that they were paid £10 by members of the 'Spinners Union of Ashton-under-Lyne' to assassinate James Ashton, Thomas' brother. However, on the night in question, James – who was the superintendent of the Apethorn Mill – was out visiting a friend and arranged for Thomas Ashton to take his place and oversee the running of the mill.

During the trial, Garside confessed to being present at the shooting but blamed Moseley for firing the gun. The jury disagreed with Garside's version of events and the judge sentenced both men to death by hanging. The execution took place shortly after nine o'clock in the morning on 25 November 1834. Their bodies were buried in the grounds of Horsemonger Lane Gaol in Surrey.

4 JANUARY 1858 An inquest was held today into the death of an old lady named Ann Mason, who died after her dress caught fire. The accident had taken place on the previous Saturday evening at her home. Mason was using a match to light a gas lamp over the fireplace, when her dress caught fire. Covered in flames, she then attempted to stagger to the front door and get help. Sadly, the flames overpowered her and she fell to the ground and died. She left behind a son and a married daughter.

5 JANUARY 1829 This week, a most distressing murder occurred in the district of Collyhurst. The victim was Catherine Cliffe, wife of papermaker James Cliffe. On the night of her death, James Cliffe left his wife to go and have a drink in the local pub. Without any food in the house to feed her or their four children, Catherine set about searching the local public houses trying to locate her husband. Whilst en route, she decided to have a few drinks herself. Sometime later she found her husband in the Kings Arms on St George's Road, where she joined him and his friends for a drink. After leaving the pub with her intoxicated husband, Catherine lit her lantern and began to escort him home. The couple were only a short distance from their house when, without reason, James Cliffe began attacking his wife, hitting and kicking her. After being challenged by a watchman, Cliffe left his injured wife to struggle home and the watchman went on his way.

Catherine entered the house shortly after her husband. Another watchman – who was walking past the address – heard a woman screaming from inside. Fearing for her safety, he managed to force his way into the property. Once inside, he witnessed Mr Cliffe hit his wife on the right side of her face, which caused her to fall and hit her head on the table. Catherine's lifeless body then slumped by the fire. The watchman told Cliffe that he would hang for his crimes, to which he showed little remorse, stating that he would only receive a short spell in prison. Appalled, the watchman left the house and went to get some assistance.

After he had departed, Cliffe left his children and the body of their mother, while he went to fetch his sister. By the time he returned, Catherine's body was cold. Her injuries were substantial: she had a fractured skull, four broken ribs, her eye was nearly forced out, and her body was black and blue.

Cliffe was later apprehended by the police and sent to the lock-up, where he admitted his crimes. At his trial, Cliffe was found guilty of the murder of his wife and sentenced to death. He was hanged on Monday, 23 March 1829 at Lancaster Castle, leaving his children orphans; they were promptly put into the workhouse.

6 JANUARY 1849 The *Manchester Guardian* reported the result of an inquest held into the death of Catherine Wiseman, the 33-year-old wife of David Wiseman. The couple lived in Reddish and had three sons; 9-year-old, Richard; 7-year-old, John and 5-year-old Fred.

On New Year's Day, Mrs Wiseman had been drinking heavily. In her drunken state, she decided to take her sons to see her husband, who was employed by Dr Charles Bell as a coachman. Once inside Dr Bell's house, she was ordered to stay in the kitchen until her husband arrived. Seeing that the wife was drunk, Dr Bell insisted that Mr Wiseman took her and the children home.

After arriving at their address, Mrs Wiseman refused to go inside and sat on the front doorstep. Angry and humiliated, Mr Wiseman picked up his wife and carried her into the kitchen and placed her on a chair. He then left and went back to Bell's house to feed the horses. On his way home, he stopped off at a local beerhouse and began to drink.

He arrived back at the family home later that evening, also now intoxicated. He walked into the kitchen, took off his boots and threw one of them at his wife. He then grabbed both boots and hit his wife across the side of the head. Catherine was not badly hurt and she managed to pick herself up and retreat to the other side of the room. However, Wiseman then grabbed a wooden cutting board – used for cutting meat – and hit his wife again, twice, across the face. After this attack, Mrs Wiseman was now bleeding. Wiseman ordered his children to bed, leaving his wife downstairs. At some point during the night, Mrs Wiseman took herself outside and fell asleep.

Mr Wiseman awoke in the early hours and discovered that his wife was still not in bed. He put on his clothes and discovered her lying on the ground outside, covered in blood. Seeing that she was very ill, he picked her up, carried her upstairs and laid her on the bed. He then turned to his son and told him to fetch his mother some brandy. Mr Wiseman then left to get help from the doctor. While walking to the house with the doctor, Mr Wiseman apologised for the state of his wife, saying he was truly ashamed. He also explained that his wife had a problem with alcohol, regularly selling their belongings to feed her addiction. Upon arriving at the house, the doctor found Mrs Wiseman taking her last breaths. He stayed with her until she passed away.

The jury at the inquest found Mr Wiseman not guilty of murder, stating that his wife had died as a result of being intoxicated and exposed to the elements. The judge issued a stark warning to Mr Wiseman, though: he had a narrow escape and another injury could have killed her. He recommended that Mr Wiseman should never drink again.

1976 A window cleaner by the name of John Jones, who lived on Hulme Hall Lane, Miles Platting, was killed after falling from the second floor of the Town Hall.

7 JANUARY 1880

One of Manchester's most infamous murders occurred on this night at the home of a wealthy man named Richard Greenwood, who lived on Westbourne Grove in Harpurhey. The victim was a 19-year-old Welsh domestic servant by the name of Sarah Jane Roberts.

The events that led to her death started early that day, when a letter was deposited through the door of Westbourne Grove. The letter was addressed to Mr Greenwood and was signed by a 'W.Wilson, Oldham Road'. The author of the note requested that Mr Greenwood should meet with him later on that day in the Three Tuns Inn, Rochdale Road, to discuss some property that the recipient owned on Queen's Road.

Mr Greenwood set off from his home at twenty-past five in the evening and headed for the public house. He waited for the man to arrive, but he never came. Westwood then left, returning home at seven o'clock. Upon his arrival, he was immediately alerted that something was wrong.

About forty-five minutes after Mr Greenwood had left the house, there had been a knock at the door; the only people in the house at the time were the maid and Mrs Greenwood. Mrs Greenwood recalled hearing the servant girl go to the door and answer it. The girl then took the visitor through the lobby and downstairs into the kitchen, closing the door behind them. Mrs Greenwood assumed that the visitor was a guest of the maid and did not think any more of it until she heard a piercing scream come from the kitchen. Alarmed, Mrs Greenwood ran to the front door and began shouting 'murder'. Her screams were heard by a neighbour, who ran into the kitchen and saw Roberts' lifeless body slumped on the floor. Her battered head was resting in a pool of blood. The back door, which had been locked, was wide open and it appeared that this was where the attacker made his escape.

The sister of the deceased believed the motive for the crime was one of passion, committed by a man from whom Roberts had declined a marriage proposal. Over the years the police interviewed several suspects; however, the murder remains unsolved.

1871 Howarth Fishwick, a 16-year-old boy of Green Lane in Failsworth, died after falling into boiling liquid while at work. The boy was employed at Wood and Wright dyers, Failsworth. He had been fixing a piece of calico when he fell into a wince machine. Fishwick was severely scalded and died later in the Royal Infirmary.

8 JANUARY 1883
This week, a woman named Mary Jane Arden from Gorton narrowly escaped death after being shot at.

On the previous Saturday evening, Mary and her brother Reuben Webster were on their way to a local beerhouse to get some ale when they bumped into Martin Henry O'Malley and his wife. Some months previous, Mary had appeared in court as a witness against O'Malley, and now he took it upon himself to seek revenge. After spotting his victim, O'Malley began to viciously verbally abuse her. Without warning he then pulled out a gun and fired straight at Mary's body. Luckily her brother managed to kick the revolver, sending the bullet away from its target. In a vain attempt to escape, Mary then fled into a local shop. O'Malley gave chase and eventually cornered his victim. He fired three more shots, hitting her in the side, left shoulder and jaw. Thinking he had killed Mary, he then left the shop and was apprehended by three passers-by and held until the police arrived. Mary was suffering from severe blood loss and was helped to her home. A surgeon attempted to extract two of the three bullets, although the bullet in her side was considered too dangerous to remove.

O'Malley's trial began on 6 February at the Liverpool Assizes. The jury listened to all of the evidence and the court found him guilty of shooting Mary. He was sentenced to twenty years' penal servitude.

9 JANUARY 1907 An inquest was held into the death of Samuel Kelshaw, who was knocked over and killed by a motorcar on Deansgate. Kelshaw was a 38-year-old carter who resided on John Street, Hulme.

On New Year's Day, he and a friend decided to go for a drink after work. At around half past five in the evening, he said goodbye to his companion on the corner of Liverpool Road. At the same time, a car being driven by Henry Hollindrake of Edgeley, Stockport, was coming around the corner. Kelshaw began to walk across the road. The driver of the car saw the carter but thought he was going to let him drive past; however, he did not, and stepped in front of the car. The car hit Kelshaw at over twenty miles per hour, knocking him to the ground. Hollindrake immediately rushed over to the injured man and helped him into his car. He then drove him to the Royal Infirmary, where he later died from his injuries.

10 JANUARY 1829 This week a shocking discovery was made in the infirmary pond. Workers at the hospital had been alerted that something was amiss in the lake because of the strange behaviour of a dog. For the previous three weeks a dog had remained at the side of the lake, howling and barking. However, the dog was removed from the pond's vicinity and the incident was forgotten.

On 3 January, a hackney coach driver was standing by the pond when he noticed something that looked like the body of a woman. The mystery lady was removed from the pond and placed in the infirmary, where it was hoped someone might identify her. She was described as being 23 years old, wearing a blue skirt, shirt and a pair of stockings. She had no bonnet and was not wearing any shoes. On her arm was a woven basket, which had the bottom missing – it was believed that this was used to weigh her body down so she did not float.

An examination of the woman revealed that she was five months pregnant and had been in the water for about three weeks. As word of the 'mystery woman' began to spread through the city, a lady came forward who lived on Quay Street and stated that she knew the victim, as she had resided with her for a short time. She was named as Winifred Hughes, daughter of a farmer from Wales. She had moved to Manchester to get a job in service. She then moved to Haslington, but came back to Manchester after realising she was pregnant. Destitute and alone, it is believed that the woman took her own life. The dog – which had loyally waited by the pond trying to attract the attention of anyone who passed by – went to live with a reverend in Yorkshire.

11 JANUARY 1905 John Jones (22), otherwise known as Martin Farrell, was today found guilty of stealing two custards and sentenced to seven days in prison. Between

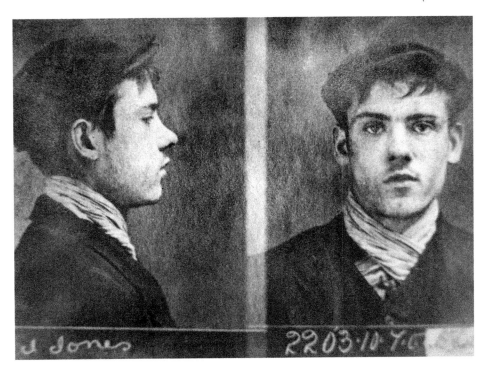

A mugshot of John James. He was described as being 6ft 1in tall with an anchor tattoo and a heart and club tattoo on the back of his right forearm. He also had some initials on his hand.

1898 and 1907, he had been convicted of stealing seven times. At the beginning of his criminal career he started off stealing food (sweets and cakes), and then moved on to more serious crimes such as housebreaking and shopbreaking.

12 JANUARY 1899 A dreadful accident occurred on this day when severe gales caused a chimney from the Standard Finishing Company, School Street, to fall upon a house, crushing the occupants and destroying their home.

On the night in question, Thomas Shawcross, a labourer who lived at No. 5 Great Newton Street, was sat down with his family for tea when, at a quarter to six in the evening, he suddenly felt his house shake. He stated that he must have blacked out because when he awoke, he could not see for debris. He managed to escape through a passage, picking up his nephew in the process. Once outside, he realised that the chimney from the factory next door had fallen on top of his home.

Trapped inside were seven members of his family. Men from the local fire station were deployed to try and rescue them from the wreckage. First out was Mrs Shawcross, who was alive but had a severe head wound and was transferred to the Royal Infirmary, where she later died. Also pulled out alive were Thomas Shawcross, their son; Eliza Howarth, their married daughter; Edith Howarth, Eliza's baby; Samuel Richardson and Sarah Richardson. The deceased were named as 19-year-old Sarah Ann Shawcross; 8-year-old Elizabeth Shawcross; 5-year-old Annie May Howarth; Sarah Ann Buckley and Mrs Shawcross, wife of Thomas. All the bodies were placed in neighbours' houses until they could be moved to the mortuary. The funerals of the five victims took place on 18 January. Hundreds gathered as the five coffins were carried to All Saints church from Newton Heath. The two coffins of the children were draped in white flowers and were carried by female mourners.

13 JANUARY 1899 An inquest took place today on the bodies of William Hodgson and John McGregor. The former was 40 years old and resided on Bowler Street, Levenshulme. McGregor was 27 years old and was a married father of four children. He lived on Aspden Street, Hulme.

The pair had been working for the City's Surveyor's Department of the Manchester Corporation when they were accidentally killed while trying to clean and repair a main sewer at the junction of City Road and Welcomb Street. The accident occurred shortly after seven o'clock in the morning, when four of the workers were instructed to enter the sewer via the manhole cover at the junction of City Road. When the men approached the cover, they noticed a strong smell coming from the sewer. Two of them decided it would be unwise to go in.

Hodgson and McGregor, however, argued that the smell posed little risk to human health and went down the manhole. Once they reached the sewer, their colleagues proceeded to follow them. After only a short distance, though, the pair seemed to stumble and then fall to the ground. Worried for their own safety, the other workers quickly raised the alarm and were lifted out of the manhole. By the time they reached the surface, they too were suffering from the effects of the poisonous gas and were barely conscious.

It took twelve attempts to rescue the two men who were still trapped in the sewer. After some time, the workers found the body of McGregor, but not Hodgson. McGregor's body was transferred to his home so his wife and four children could arrange an appropriate burial. The body of William Hodgson was discovered four days later on the grid of a sewer in Davyhulme. It was believed that his body had washed there with the flow of sewerage. At the inquest, the coroner ruled that the two men had died as a result of being poisoned from toxic gases. Although the coroner could not find anyone to blame for their deaths, the Corporation did offer compensation to the families of the deceased men.

14 JANUARY 1925 This was the week that 3-year-old Harold Cartledge died as a result of being severely scalded. On the previous Saturday evening, his mother was preparing a bath at their home on Ashton New Road when Harold accidentally fell into the hot water. He was transferred to Booth Hall Hospital, where he died two days later of his injuries.

At the inquest, the coroner issued a stark warning to parents to ensure that they filled the bath with cold water first, so this kind of incident would not happen again.

15 JANUARY 1749 In January, the heads of Adjutant Thomas Syddall, Captain Thomas Theodorus Deacon and Lieutenant Chadwick, all of them officers in the Manchester Regiment, were stolen

The Manchester Exchange, 1835.

from the top of the Exchange. Their heads had been on display at the Exchange since 4 August, the officers having been executed after being found guilty of high treason.

1930 A painter by the name of John Carrol died on this day while painting the staircase of a building next to the Piccadilly Picture Theatre. Carrol was 39 years old and lived on Brampton Street, Ardwick. His head was hit a by a lift, crushing his skull and breaking his neck.

16 JANUARY 1919 An enquiry was held today into the deaths of Captain Charles Adrian Brown and Private Cornelius Joseph Cafferty, both of whom were killed in a flying accident near Alexandra Park.

Captain Brown, the 23-year-old son of a lieutenant serving with the Royal Air Corps, was a local lad; he lived on Daisy Bank Road. He had played an active role in the First World War, flying with the bomber squadron. The day before the Armistice was declared, his plane was hit and he was slightly injured. He returned to Manchester to recuperate.

On 16 January, Brown was testing a new plane at the Aeroplane Acceptance Park when three wounded soldiers from the nearby hospital asked if they could travel with him. The captain stated that he could only take one passenger, and Cafferty was chosen to take the trip. Once the men were safely on board, Brown attempted to take off. The plane was only a few metres from the ground when it appeared to turn on its side and overturn. It then crashed to the ground. Moments later, the petrol tank burst into flames and within a few seconds the plane was engulfed in a fireball. Staff at the aerodrome rushed to put out the flames but it took two hours before this was accomplished and the plane was cool enough for the bodies to be removed.

The body of Private Cafferty was transferred back to Lancaster, where his wife arranged his burial. On 18 January 1919, Captain Brown was buried in a private Roman Catholic grave at Southern Cemetery, Chorlton.

17 JANUARY 1883 On this night, a terrible fire broke out at the home of Joseph Levenstein. Joseph, his wife and four children lived on Park Street in Cheetham. Shortly after half past seven in the evening, Mrs Levenstein awoke to find her house full of smoke. She rushed to rescue her two children, who were sleeping in a small room upstairs. Isaac – her second youngest child – had managed to make his way to the top of the stairs. She grabbed him and carried him outside before attempting to re-enter the house to rescue her youngest son, but the heat and the smoke stopped her from getting back inside. Two policemen, who were passing the house, managed to get a ladder and tried to save the youngster by smashing the back window. The men managed to gain entry into the child's room but the young boy was already dead. Isaac was transferred to the infirmary, where it was hoped that he would live.

18 JANUARY 1905 Joseph Watson, an employee at the Gresham Packing House, Thirlby Street, Chorlton-on-Medlock, was killed on this day whilst at work. Watson was talking to a fellow employee whilst operating the hoist on the fifth storey of the building when he lost his footing and slipped. Such was the severity of the fall that Watson died instantly.

19 JANUARY 1880 A gang of pickpockets who usually operated in Birmingham decided to leave their usual patch and come to Manchester. They managed to go undetected for a few months, but were caught midway through the year and sentenced to three months in prison.

A mugshot of Thomas Nelson, caught pickpocketing in Manchester.

20 JANUARY 1904 A dreadful electric car accident that resulted in the death of a married man named Thomas Burn occurred this week on Deansgate.

On the previous Saturday, Burn had been employed by Salford Council to monitor the departure and arrival of cars. Shortly before his death he was stood between two stationary cars, having a discussion with one of the drivers, when a third car came speeding from the direction of King Street and crashed into the car in front of him, crushing him in the process. Burn was transferred to the infirmary, where he later died. The driver of the vehicle stated that ice from the recent bad weather had made the rails slippery, and that when he pressed his foot on the sandpipe, his car skidded and he was unable to avoid the collision.

21 JANUARY 1837 Mr James Esdale, a hat manufacturer who lived on New Stretford Road, was recovering at home after being the victim of a highway robbery. On the previous Sunday morning he had been travelling along Stretford Road when

Deansgate. The scene of a tragic car accident that resulted in the death of Thomas Burn.

he was attacked from behind by a group of men who repeatedly hit him over the head with iron bars. While he lay injured on the ground, one of the attackers put their hand over his mouth to stop him shouting. The same man then used the victim's own stock to try to strangle him. As this was happening, another attacker began to raid the victim's pockets and stole a purse containing twenty sovereigns. Once they had got the money, the assailants then fled across the adjoining fields. After picking himself up, the victim began shouting 'murder' and a watchman came to his aid.

Two men were later charged with highway robbery, but they were acquitted at the subsequent trial at the Liverpool Assizes. The true perpetrators were never caught.

22 JANUARY 1866 A serious incident occurred shortly before two o'clock in the afternoon at Liverpool Road Station, when the roof collapsed while it was being erected. It is believed that an unsecured girder caused the roof to give way, which resulted in the loss of two lives and injured a further twenty-nine men who were also working at the station. Seventeen of the men were seriously injured. Their injuries included fractured skulls, cuts, broken bones and amputations. The two victims that died were Thomas Sherwood, a joiner of Bridgewater Street and Mark Russell, a 35-year-old bricklayer of Syndall Street.

23 JANUARY 1874 An inquest was held on this day into the death of George Matthews, who was run over by a train. Matthews was a 65-year-old clerk, who resided at Adlands Lane, Levenshulme.

On the day of his death, he was attempting to step off a moving train in Levenshulme when he lost his footing and fell between the carriage and the track. Matthews was unable to get out of the way in time and a section of the train ran over him, crushing his body and causing serious injuries. He was transferred to the Royal Infirmary, where he died the following day. The jury returned a verdict of accidental death.

24 JANUARY 1879 At the City Police Court, Mary Ryves – niece of Sir Harry Smith – was sentenced to twelve months in prison for the cruel treatment of two children who had been left in her care at the Orphan Home in Strangeways. Thomas Holland had entrusted Ryves, the founder of the home, with the care of 9-year-old Ada and 11-year-old Alice Holland. Thomas had agreed to pay 5s per week for her to care for his children. When his payments became irregular, the children complained of being mistreated, accusing Ryves of beating them with a poker, and feeding them on bread and water, leaving them emaciated.

25   JANUARY 1926   A tramline point cleaner by the name of Peter Rowe was working at the junction of Portland Street and Oxford Road when he was hit by a cab. The cab appeared to have been driving at twenty-five to thirty miles per hour and hit Rowe from behind. The wheels crushed his body as they rolled over his back. Rowe was still alive when he was transported to the Royal Infirmary. He managed to mutter a few words to his father, before he passed away as a result of his injuries.

26   JANUARY 1923   An inquest was held today on the body of 7-year-old Samuel Jones. Jones had been walking with 12-year-old John Lees near Oswald Street when the pair decided to cross the road. Lees told Jones not to cross as he did not think it was safe to do so, but the little lad slipped past him and ran into the road. Coming down the road in his motorcar was company director Henry Jefferies. As Jefferies approached Oswald Street, the young lad ran in front of his car and was instantly knocked to the floor. Jones later died of his injuries. The coroner ruled that the driver of the car could not have done anything to avoid the accident and returned a verdict of accidental death.

27   JANUARY 1927   This week an errand boy was delivering parcels in Manchester when a lorry travelling on King Street West struck him, causing serious injuries and leading to his death. The driver of the lorry was named as Ralph Swindells from Macclesfield. At the inquest he stated that he had turned to miss some stationary traffic and did not see the victim. The coroner ruled that the death was accidental but instructed Swindells to ensure that in future his lorry had a mirror fitted so he could see what was behind him.

28   JANUARY 1867   On this day, four men were killed while working at the Lancashire and Yorkshire Railway Company, situated on Junction Street, Miles Platting. The four men were named as 19-year-old Charles Flannery; 42-year-old John Cooper; 39-year-old Charles Copestake and 32-year-old John Reid.

The men had been using a hoist to load a truck full of timber onto a carriage when one of the chains attached to the hoist snapped, sending the heavy truck and its contents crashing to the ground. Several men who were working underneath the hoist were instantly crushed, and a rescue operation was launched in an effort to rescue the trapped workers. Three men were found dead at the scene and another seven were injured. One man died later at the Royal Infirmary.

The inquest was held a week later and the jury ruled that the deaths were accidental. The coroner finished the proceedings by stating that the chains supporting the hoist were not strong enough to carry the weight of the trunk. He recommended that from that day forward the hoist should not be fully dependent on chains and a catch system should be implemented to stop such an incident from happening again.

29 JANUARY 1908 On this day the *Manchester Guardian* reported on the shocking story of 40-year-old Mary Ann Shea, who was brutally hacked to death by her husband. The event occurred in the early hours of the previous morning, at their lodging house on Parker Street, which was situated off Wilmott Street. It appeared that some time between one and two o'clock, Mrs Shea and her husband William had a quarrel. Without warning he grabbed his axe and began assaulting his wife. After the crime had been committed, Mr Shea took himself to the police station and handed himself in. By the time the police arrived at the house, the victim was lying in a pool of blood with serious wounds to her head and body. She was then transferred to the infirmary, where it was expected that she would not survive.

30 JANUARY 1856 Two Manchester newspapers reported on the exhumation of the body of John Monaghan from St Wilfred's Roman Catholic chapel, Hulme. John was born in Ireland in 1786 and had married his wife Ann by 1820; the couple went on to have five children. In the late 1830s, John and his family left Ireland to seek a better life in in Manchester, which was enjoying the rewards of the Industrial Revolution. John quickly found work as a tailor and set up home in a modest terrace house in Chorlton-upon-Medlock.

In June 1855, John decided to take out a life insurance policy that would pay his son £300 upon his death. Two months after he took out the policy, John sadly died of 'alleged' natural causes. He was interred in a public grave in St Wilfred's churchyard. Shortly after his death, his son James Monaghan put in a claim to receive his father's insurance payout. Their suspicions aroused, the insurance company decided to carry out their own investigations and concluded that John had been murdered by poison for his life insurance claim. Believing that there was enough evidence for a trial, the police arrested James and three acquaintances. The body of John Monaghan had already been buried, so a request was submitted to the city coroner, Mr Herford, for the body to be exhumed. Mr Herford granted the disinterment and five excavators set out to locate the body of Monaghan.

With no headstones on public graves and with the large number of people interred in these plots, locating the body was an arduous task. After three days, the body was finally discovered. There had been a delay of five and half months between the interment and exhumation, meaning that decomposition had started to break down the body. Disinfectant was used to try and block out the odour that was being released from the corpse. Considering the amount of time the body had been dead, it was surprisingly recognisable: the coroner observed that the deceased male was roughly 60 years old and was bald; he also noted that the eyes of the corpse were badly decomposed. The undertaker, who had known the deceased for over sixteen years, also verified the identity of the dead man. A series of medical tests were carried out on the corpse and, two weeks later, it was revealed by the coroner that John Monaghan had died of dysentery and diarrhoea. The coroner then passed the verdict that John had died of 'natural causes'. James Monaghan and his acquaintances were acquitted of all charges.

1926   The *Manchester Guardian* reported on this day that nine people had been killed in January on the city's streets, as a result of being knocked down by cars and waggons.

31   **JANUARY** **1555**   On this day, a native of Manchester named John Bradford was found guilty of being a heretic and sentenced to death. Born in 1510 into a wealthy family, Bradford had a privileged upbringing and, in later life, studied law. At the age of 38, he left the legal profession and took up theology. Nicknamed 'Holy Bradford', he was ordained as a chaplain for the Church of England and travelled around the North West of England preaching sermons.

In 1553, Edward VI died, along with the Church of England. His successor was Mary I, who was a devote follower of the Catholic Church and arrested anyone who did not follow her religion. Bradford refused to convert. He was subsequently arrested and held at the Tower of London.

At nine o'clock in the morning, on 1 July 1855, he was burned at the stake at Smithfield, London. Sharing the stake was another man called John Leaf. Before the stake was lit, it is said that Bradford turned to Leaf and said, 'Be of good comfort, brother, for we shall have a happy supper with the Lord tonight'.

1852   Patrick McDermott was sat in his cell awaiting trial for the wilful murder of a man named Hughes. The events unfolded on the morning of 16 January, at a pub called The Fox situated on Deansgate. Hughes and a man named Cunningham were drinking in the vault when they got into a fight. The fight was broken up by a group of men who were also drinking in the pub, so the squabbling pair then decided to go outside. Once outside, they began to square up to each other. At the same time, McDermott was leaving the pub, carrying a brick. Without warning he threw the brick at Hughes, hitting him on the side of the forehead. The victim fell to the floor and was transferred to the infirmary, where he died two weeks later.

The inquest was held on 30 January and the jury found McDermott guilty of the wilful murder of Hughes. He was then transferred to the assizes, where he would stand trial.

FEBRUARY

1 FEBRUARY 1859 A married woman named Ellen Robinson was at her home on Albert Street when she got into an argument with her husband, William, the landlord of the Cross Keys beerhouse. The couple regularly argued and it often ended in a brawl. William Robinson enjoyed a drink and on the day in question he had returned home from a funeral a little worse for wear. The couple began quarrelling and then fighting. Filled with rage, Robinson began attacking his wife. According to medical experts, he used a knife and thrust it into her neck four times in an attack so brutal that the woman died instantly, her blood oozing through the floorboards (bloodstains were found on the floor below). After the attack, William took his time to clean the crime scene. He then went to visit his daughter in Longsight and stated that he was heartbroken because he wife was having an affair. He pleaded with his daughter to go back to the beerhouse with him, but she refused as she was baking a cake.

Robinson then left his daughter and went home. After entering his house, he attempted to burn it down by releasing the gas and lighting the fires. He then went upstairs and placed a ladder at the top of the staircase, attached a piece of rope to a nail and jumped. He died instantly. The couple's daughter discovered the bodies of her parents later that day after returning from work.

2 FEBRUARY 1876 A woman named Jane Lomas appeared at the City Police Court charged with selling rabbits at the Manchester Market that were unfit for human consumption.

The incident had occurred on New Year's Eve. Inspector Atkinson passed the market and noticed that Lomas did not have a stall. When he approached her, he spotted that she was selling rabbits from a barrel. Upon opening the barrel, he was greeted by the sight of four putrid rabbits that were green in colour. In the barrel were several rabbit skins that were also rancid. Lomas claimed to have bought the rabbits from a fish dealer who also had a stall on the market. She was fined £5 and costs and informed that if she could not afford to pay the fine, she would be sentenced to one month in prison.

3 FEBRUARY 1831 On this day a maid named Mary Harris, who had been in service with the Blackley family, was found to have stolen various items from the house. When the crime occurred, Mr and Mrs Blackley were attending a funeral. They returned home in the evening and discovered that a silk scarf, a velvet bonnet, dresses and caps with a value of £30 were missing. The servant was later found at a lodging house in Bank Top: the owner of the establishment had called the police after discovering the stolen items in her possession. Mary was then apprehended and sent to the lock-up to await trial.

4 FEBRUARY 1826 On this day, the people of Manchester were awaking to the distressing news that a murder had been committed at a mill on Marsden Street. The victim was a fustian manufacturer named Mr Price.

The incident had occurred at one o'clock in the afternoon on the previous day. Mr Greaves – who occupied the warehouse next door – was eating his lunch when he saw smoke coming from the upper saleroom of Mr Price's warehouse. Greaves, aided by some passers-by, attempted to gain entry into the saleroom but was unable to access the building for twenty minutes because the door was locked. When the group eventually got inside, they noticed that the door had been blocked with pieces of fustian. The floor was also covered with the fabric. As they began removing the cloth, they discovered the head and then the body of Mr Price. The material covering the victim was full of blood and fragments of brain.

The body was taken to the infirmary, were it was confirmed that Mr Price died from three distinct wounds to the head, which were probably caused by an axe. One of the wounds had penetrated the skull and entered the brain.

Suspicion immediately fell on an employee of Mr Price named James Evans, who had been seen by a fellow worker going into the saleroom with Price. He was also spotted with blood on his shirt, which he claimed was from carrying the body of his master, but it was later revealed that he had never carried or touched the deceased man after he was taken from the warehouse.

The subsequent trial at the Lancaster Assizes appeared to be cut and dried, as far as the Manchester media were concerned. The trial began on the morning of 17 March and by late afternoon – to the shock of the crowd and local media – Evans was acquitted.

The perpetrator was never caught. Evans' trial had made him famous in Manchester, but it was not long before he was back in custody, charged with attempting to steal books from a shop in Salford. He was found guilty and sentenced to three months' hard labour on the treadmill.

5 FEBRUARY 1887 An 18-year-old 'scuttler' by the name of Joseph Brady had been out drinking with two women when he ended up in an argument with a member of a rival gang called Burns. He and Brady ended up having a short-lived scuffle outside the former's house, and the pair separated and carried on with their night. Once Brady had left, Burns gathered a dozen friends and turned up at the house where Brady and the two women were staying. Burns and his gang banged on the door and urged Brady to come out and fight. He refused and the gang began to kick in the front door, at which point Brady ran to the door to try and stop them, but it was too late and they were now inside the house. Upon seeing Brady, a gang member named Owen Callaghan pulled out a knife and began stabbing him repeatedly in the chest and abdomen, leaving him in a pool of blood. The gang then fled. Joseph Brady died almost instantly. Burns and seven other 'scuttlers' were sent for trial at the assizes.

The trial began on 5 May and lasted for two days. Burns was acquitted, but Callaghan was found guilty of manslaughter and sentenced to twenty years' penal servitude.

6 FEBRUARY 1886 John Moss, owner of the Masons Arms beerhouse in Upper Medlock Street, was charged at the City Police Court with attempting to murder his wife. It appears that on evening before the incident the couple had been arguing, which led his wife to leave their marital bed and sleep in a different room with her children. The following morning, in a jealous rage, Mr Moss went downstairs and picked up a razor, went into the room where his wife was sleeping with his children and crept over to her usual bed. What he could not see in the dark was that the beds had been moved, and his 9-year-old daughter Lilly was in the bed that his wife usually slept in. Mr Moss stabbed at the bed, believing the sleeping body was his wife, who awoke and attempted to fend off her husband, receiving a brutal attack in the process. Bleeding, she managed to escape with her children into the street, only to be followed and knocked down by her husband. Mrs Moss began screaming 'Murder, murder!' and a number of people began came to her aid.

Mrs Moss and her daughter were taken to hospital suffering from stab wounds and loss of blood. Lilly had three minor injuries and was expected to make a full recovery. Mrs Moss was not so lucky; she had sustained a stab wound behind her ear that had caused severe blood loss. Doctors were so concerned about Mrs Moss' condition that they were unable to confirm if she would survive her injuries. However, some days later Mrs Moss made a full recovery and her husband was charged with attempted murder. He was sentenced at the Spring Assizes to twelve years in prison for wounding with intent to commit grievous bodily harm.

7 FEBRUARY 1896 The city coroner held an inquest on this day, into the death of a 2-year-old boy named Hallam. The young boy was at his parents' home on Hyde Road when he found a beer bottle in one of the bedrooms and drank the contents. In an instant the child became sick and a short time later, died. His parents revealed that the contents of the bottle contained the deadly poison carbolic acid.

The coroner condemned the parents for keeping the acid in an unmarked bottle, stating that in the past twelve months he had seen thirty cases of carbolic poisoning. The jury ruled that the death was accidental.

8 FEBRUARY 1882 On this evening, Mary Bouch was at home with her 4-year-old child when her husband Benjamin Bouch arrived with her two older sons – John, aged 10, and James, aged 7. Mary had not seen her husband since before Christmas, when the family were let out of the workhouse. It appeared that the father

was struggling to look after the children and had been begging in the streets in an attempt to feed them.

Mary had managed to turn her life around since her spell in the workhouse and had got a job at the local mill. Benjamin asked her to look after the two boys but she refused, stating that she already had a child to care for and was sleeping on a table with shavings because she could not afford any furniture. The father then left with the boys and told his wife that she would never see them again.

At half past seven in the evening, Benjamin took the two boys to the bank of the Rochdale Canal near Union Street, and threw them both in. He was apprehended a short time later. The body of James was recovered at twenty past eight. John was not found until five past twelve on the next morning. Bouch was sentenced to death at the Manchester Assizes for the murder of his children. The sentence was later reduced after the Home Secretary intervened, arguing that Benjamin had committed the act because he was in a state of extreme poverty and acted in desperation.

9 FEBRUARY 1843 Two men and three women were brought up at the Borough Court, charged with stealing several items from the home of a cotton spinner named Mr Sharn.

The burglary had taken place the previous Saturday night in Cross Street. Sharn and his wife had left their address after dinner to go to the local market. While they were out it was alleged that William Walsh, James Lynch and his three sisters broke into the house using a crowbar and stole a writing desk, a Chinese scent box and items of clothes, worth a total of £4.

Shortly after ten o'clock on the same evening, two passing policemen noticed that a chimney was on fire at the house where James Lynch and his sisters lived. The policemen entered the house and found a section of the writing desk under the bed of one of the sisters. They also discovered a special farthing and the scent box, which belonged to the victim. The men then searched the pockets of James Lynch, who was in bed, and found black sealing wax that corresponded with wax from Sharn's writing desk. After the evidence was heard, Walsh and Lynch were sent for trial, where they were later acquitted.

10 FEBRUARY 1853 An inquest was held on his day into the death of 64-year-old John Quinn, who died at the Manchester Workhouse. Two days previous, in the early hours of the morning, a police constable found the man drunk and asleep, snoring very loudly. Noticing his workhouse clothing, the constable transported the man to the workhouse infirmary to sober up. Later that day, one of the nurses became concerned with Quinn's health and called for the surgeon. Sadly, he died the following day. The post-mortem revealed that there was no alcohol in his system, but there was evidence to suggest that he was intoxicated when he was brought into the workhouse. The surgeon based his theory on a number of large fish bones in the stomach that, he stated, would not have been digested while sober. It was further argued that if Quinn had been seen when he was first admitted to the infirmary, he could have been saved. The jury found that the man had died from exposure, which had been aggravated by a failure to seek medical advice.

11 FEBRUARY 1836 A woman named Ann Maxwell appeared at the New Bailey, charged with stealing goods from her employer, Mr Doubleday, a wealthy gentleman who resided in Strangeways and who had employed Maxwell as a cook. Without his knowledge, she helped herself to candles, soap, sugar, waistcoat patterns and other items. After stealing the goods, she arranged for her nephew – a man named Thomas Hambleton – to collect them and take them to be sold. The plan was going well until a police officer caught her nephew with the goods on King Street. The boy admitted getting the bundle from his aunt and she was later arrested. Maxwell admitted her guilt and Mrs Doubleday confirmed that the items belonged to her. After hearing the evidence, the judge committed Maxwell for trial.

12 FEBRUARY 1848 On this day, a shocking explosion occurred, killing thirteen people, all of whom were under the age of 20. The youngest victim was Samuel Wadsworth, who was only 2 years old. He died along with his 7-year-old brother John. The incident occurred at Thomas Riley's factory on Medlock Street. The explosion was blamed on a faulty boiler that, the coroner stated, had not been maintained correctly. Mr Riley was held accountable for the accident and he was taken into custody.

13 FEBRUARY 1834 A 3-year-old boy died after he mistakenly drank some poison. The boy was the son of Mr Tudor, a shoemaker who lived in Harpurhey. While at home he picked up a bottle that contained arsenic, thinking it was a drink. The surgeon was immediately called and the boy's stomach was pumped, but it was too late and he died in a matter of hours.

14 FEBRUARY 1889 An inquest was held on the body of a 9-week-old boy in Liverpool. The child had been discovered in a tin box at Lime Street Station, which had arrived on a train from Manchester and ended up in the goods department. The box was addressed to a 'Mrs Cranworth'. A clerk named Evans was alerted that something was wrong when he heard a noise coming from inside. He managed to open the box and found the child asleep.

The infant was then sent to the workhouse, where he later died. Enquiries were made and it was found that the child was the illegitimate son of 24-year-old Elizabeth Porter and 27-year-old John Fenton, who lived in Ardwick. Porter admitted her guilt and the pair were sent to the Liverpool Assizes on a charge of manslaughter. Their trial was held on 9 March. After hearing the evidence, the jury found the pair guilty. Fenton was sentenced to five years in prison and Elizabeth to eight months for the manslaughter of their child.

15 FEBRUARY 1871 Margaret Madden, 18, was in prison on this day after being found guilty of stealing. Between 1871 and 1912, Margaret would receive twenty-six convictions in Manchester – six of which were for stealing. She often used aliases; the image shows Margaret in custody, having been arrested under the name Catherine Madden.

16 FEBRUARY 1914 An inquest was held today into the death of 4-year-old Francis Jeffers, who died after drowning in the Rochdale Canal. The young boy was the son of William Jeffers, who lived on Thorpe Road, Newton Heath. The boy's father had first reported him missing on the previous Tuesday. His mother said that

Margaret Madden, who sometimes went by the alias Catherine Madden.

he had been playing in the street with his brother when she saw him talking to a youth aged 15. The mother walked into the kitchen and when she returned, she noticed that both of her sons were missing. After a quick search she found her youngest son on Oldham Road, but Francis was missing. Along with neighbours, the Jeffers began to search the local neighbourhood. Mr Jeffers even offered a reward of £10 to anyone who had information regarding the disappearance of his son, but it was all in vain. The body of Francis Jeffers was discovered in the canal five days later.

The jury at the inquest ruled that the boy died from drowning. There were no marks on the body to suggest foul play, but they could not state how he ended up in the canal.

17 FEBRUARY 1888 This week, 4-year-old Samuel Renshaw died while at school. Samuel lived with his parents on Back Water Street, which was off Portland Street.

The tragic death occurred on the previous Thursday afternoon at St Chad's School in Cheetham. Just as the children were leaving their classrooms, the stone steps leading from the girls' school to the outside collapsed, crushing five of them. Teachers from the boys' school ran over and assisted in removing the stone slabs in an attempt to release the trapped youngsters. Sadly, Samuel was already dead by the time he was rescued. A large stone slab had landed directly on top of him, crushing him to death. The children that had survived were sent by cab to the Royal Infirmary. The body of Samuel Renshaw, meanwhile, was transferred to the mortuary at the Clinical Hospital, York Street.

The coroner at the inquest reported that the death was accidental but he insisted that all the steps surrounding the school should be checked to make sure they were safe, to avoid a similar tragedy occurring.

18 FEBRUARY 1843 This week a widow named Grace Williams died after accidentally setting herself on fire at her home on Goulden Street.

19 FEBRUARY 1889 On this day, an 18-year-old man named Charles Parton entered the shop of a Mr Bromley – a chemist who resided on London Road, Liverpool – and stole a pound of chloral, a sedative commonly used in the nineteenth century to treat insomnia.

A week later, a wealthy paper merchant named John Fletcher, who lived in Southport and was chairman of the Southport Conservative Club, was in Manchester conducting some business on Cannon Street. After finishing his business he went for a drink in the Mitre Hotel, leaving shortly before five o'clock. He was then seen on Victoria Street talking to Charles Parton. The two men then went to the Three Arrows on Deansgate. They stayed there for a short time, before getting into a cab and instructing the driver to go to Stretford Road. As the cab passed Cavendish Road, Parton got out his chloral and drugged Mr Fletcher. He then stole the man's watch, chain and purse, and fled by opening the door and jumping out of the moving cab.

A group of people who were walking past the cab on Cavendish Road alerted the driver to the cab door being open. When the driver went to check, he found Fletcher slumped forward, unconcious. A police officer ordered the driver to take Fletcher to the infirmary, where he died later that day.

Parton was subsequently arrested and tried at the Liverpool Assizes on 18 and 19 March, where he was found guilty of the murder and robbery of John Fletcher and sentenced to death. However, Parton was never sent to the gallows: the following month, the Home Secretary commuted the sentence to life in prison, on the grounds that he was unaware of the strength of the drug when he administered it.

Parton was released from Dartmoor Prison in 1904 and moved to Bath, where he found employment as a market salesman. In 1925, he was sent to prison again for three months' hard labour after being found guilty of pickpocketing a woman in Southampton. He was by this time 57 years old and married, with young children.

20 **FEBRUARY** 1871 The city coroner – a man named Edward Herford – held a post-mortem on the body of a 1-month-old baby who died from poisoning. The child was the son of a lurryman named William Moores, who lived with his family on Medlock Street.

The events that led to the baby's death began on the previous Thursday, when he would not stop crying. Fearing something was wrong, his mother went to a neighbour for help. The neighbour suggested giving the child five drops of laudanum, which Mrs Moores mixed with sugar, diluting it with water. After administering it to the child, he began convulsing and died the following day. The coroner ruled that the child's death was accidental.

21 **FEBRUARY** 1866 This week, a 6-year-old girl named Elizabeth Cottam died whilst playing with some other children near her house on Frances Street, Strangeways. Elizabeth was sat on top of a handcart that was being pushed by some children, when it suddenly flipped over and threw them on the road. Elizabeth died almost instantly. The jury ruled that her death was accidental, although they were of the opinion that the owner of the handcart should contribute to her funeral.

22 **FEBRUARY** 1908 The *Manchester Guardian* reported on the tragic murder of a man named James McCraw, and the attempted murder of his sister, Charlotte Ann Ramsbottom. The incident had occurred in the early hours of the previous day at the Prince of Wales beerhouse in Gorton.

It appears that just after midnight, Charlotte was arguing with her husband John in the beerhouse owned by her mother. Upon hearing the commotion, Charlotte's mother and brother went to intervene. As they entered the room, John fired a bullet into his wife's chest. He then pointed the gun at his wife's brother and shot twice, hitting him in the arm and stomach. James later died. Charlotte survived her wounds and gave evidence at a subsequent inquest.

John was arrested at his mother's house in Openshaw. He was sent to trial on 23 April, at the Manchester Assizes. After hearing evidence from the defence and prosecution, the jury took just minutes to find the prisoner guilty and he was sentenced him to death. John's supporters attempted to get a reprieve by putting together a petition to Herbert Gladstone, the Home Secretary, which stated that he was demented at the time of the crime. The petition contained over 20,000 signatures and included the names of the coroner's jury. John's elderly mother also wrote a heartfelt letter to Mr Gladstone pleading for her son's life, but the Home Secretary refused to grant the reprieve. John Ramsbottom was executed on 12 May at Manchester. According to reports, he enjoyed a hearty breakfast and walked calmly to the scaffold.

23 FEBRUARY 1868 Two bodies were discovered in the Rochdale Canal, near Chorlton Street. The bodies were identified as Thomas Royle, who lived on Higher Ormond Street, and 21-year-old Elizabeth Gillard, who resided with her parents at a house on Portland Street. A witness stated that the couple were engaged and had last been sighted together on the previous Saturday evening.

Royle had been visiting Gillard at her home when, sometime after nine o'clock, the young girl decided to accompany her fiancé part of the way home. It is believed that while they were walking by the canal, one of them fell into the water and a rescue attempt was made that resulted in the deaths of the young couple.

Both bodies were transferred to the Mechanics Arms, where they awaited a post-mortem. At the inquest, the jury found no evidence of foul play and returned a verdict of 'found drowned'.

24 FEBRUARY 1851 On this day, an Irishman named John Smith, who resided in Liverpool, was brought up at the Borough Court charged with stealing a teapot. Smith was a petty thief who regularly travelled to Manchester to steal.

At around noon on the previous Saturday, he was walking along Great Jackson Street and came across a broker shop owned by a Mr Bailey. In the window was a metal teapot. Smith walked up to the window and helped himself to the teapot before fleeing the scene. Mrs Bailey, who witnessed the crime, gave chase and eventually caught the culprit, who handed back the teapot and admitted his guilt. As Smith had been charged twice with theft in Manchester before, the judge committed him for trial at the next sessions. The trial was held on 22 March 1851. He was found guilty and sentenced to ten years' transportation.

25 FEBRUARY 1914 The first serious accident on the electric tramway occurred on this morning. The tramcar was at full capacity, carrying forty passengers. It was doing its usual route from Slade Lane to the city when it overturned whilst travelling around a sharp bend at the corner of High Street and Upper Brook Street. Some passengers managed to escape by smashing the glass windows; however, others remained trapped in the wreckage. Workmen in a nearby street dashed to the scene with crowbars to try and help the trapped passengers. All the injured passengers were then transferred to the infirmary. It was concluded that the accident was caused by the driver taking the bend too fast in foggy weather.

26 FEBRUARY 1897 Emily Jane Porter and a mineral water manufacturer called Henry James Worth were acquitted of poisoning their two children, Charles Harold and Henry James. The 8-week-old twin boys were found dead in their beds on 25 January. An autopsy was held on the bodies and it was concluded that the children had died as a result of being poisoned. The parents were found to have administered the poison and were transferred to the Manchester Assizes.

When the trial was heard at court, specialists were brought in to examine the children's bottles and re-examine their bodies to see if they could find any evidence to suggest that the children had been murdered. The results varied, but no one could definitively state that the children had been poisoned. The jury therefore ruled that there was insufficient evidence to charge the couple. The pair were acquitted by the judge.

27 FEBRUARY 1924 On this day, 28-year-old Francis William Brooker of Greenheys, Manchester, was sentenced to death for the murder of 14-year-old Percy Sharpe.

Percy Sharpe was born in 1910. He was the eldest child of Percy and Ellen Elizabeth Sharpe, who resided in Ardwick. At a quarter to nine in the morning on 4 September 1923, Percy left his home to visit the Juvenile Labour Exchange in Queen Street, Manchester. Labour exchanges were set up in 1909 to help the unemployed find work. Percy never reached the exchange. While on Oxford Street he met Francis Brooker, who persuaded him to get into his car on the premise of finding him employment. The exact events of what happened next are somewhat unclear, but Percy was next seen at twenty past two by a platelayer named James Oswald Hetherington, who was employed by the Cheshire Lines Committee. Hetherington was working on the railway about half a mile from the Northenden junction when he heard screams coming from Carrs Wood. On approaching the junction, he was alerted to a young boy who was in a state of undress and was covered in blood, shouting that he was dying. The boy cried out that he had been stabbed in the back. Hetherington promptly carried Percy to a local school in Northenden, where he was then transferred to Stepping Hill Hospital. He later died of his wounds.

Shortly after the murder a local man was arrested; however, an inquest acquitted the man on the grounds of insufficient evidence. It would be another three months before Brooker was arrested. He very nearly got away with the crime, as he was only arrested after his home was searched for an unrelated incident and the belongings of Percy Sharpe were discovered. The police found the boy's trousers wrapped in brown paper in his bath, while they also found Percy's diary and labour exchange card in a box. In Brooker's allotment they found the young boy's braces wrapped in a newspaper. Brooker was arrested and held in custody until his trial.

The trial was held at the Manchester Assizes and lasted for two days. The jury made up of ten men and two women found the accused guilty of the wilful murder of 14-year-old Percy Sharpe and on 27 February 1924, Francis William Brooker was sentenced to death for his crime.

28 FEBRUARY 1888 John Alfred Gell was in the dock charged with the murder of Mary Miller and the attempted murder of her daughter, Isabella. The murder occurred on the previous Thursday at the home of the victim. Isabella Miller had got into an argument with Gell – who had been lodging with the two women in Moston – after she asked him to leave. He had been staying with the Millers since before Christmas, but he was no longer working or attempting to get work.

After hearing the argument, Mary also asked Gell to leave; an argument broke out between the pair and he picked up an axe and struck her on the head with such force that the axe lodged in her skull. Isabella was also attacked by Gell but was still alive.

After committing the crime Gell attempted to flee, but was chased by a police officer and eventually gave himself up. Whilst in custody, he stated that he was in love with Mary, who was separated from her husband, and claimed that she had promised to let him lodge with her until he could find employment. Gell further argued that his relationship with Mary was fine until Isabella moved in and asked him to leave because she was jealous. It appears that after murdering Mary, Gell contemplated taking his own life, so they could be together in heaven.

On 21 April 1888, he was sentenced to death at the Manchester Assizes. He was executed shortly before eight o'clock on 15 May at Strangeways prison. Before the executioner – Berry of Bradford – performed his duties, Gell shouted, 'Isabella Miller, I die an innocent man!' A white cap was then placed over his head and with the noose firmly in place he was dropped five feet and remained there for an hour. His body was then removed and buried within the precinct of the prison.

MARCH

1 MARCH 1912 On this day, the daughters of David Jones – a pipelayer who worked for the Manchester Corporation – appeared at the Manchester County Court in an attempt to claim compensation for the loss of their father.

On 10 October 1910, David had been laying pipes at the corner of Moss Lane East and Wilmslow Road when a horse spooked and fell down into the pit, crushing him. The horse died instantly, but David was brought out alive. He was treated for six months for the effects of shock, and after this period he began to do some light work for the council. Since the accident, his daughters argued that he had suffered twice with bronchitis and had died in January. The judged ruled that the cause of his death was bronchitis, which had nothing to do with the accident; he therefore refused compensation to the two sisters.

2 MARCH 1887 An inquest was held on the body of a 2-year-old girl named Nina Gough, who had died the previous Tuesday at her home on Dalton Street. The cause of her death was recorded as phosphorus poisoning. Her parents revealed that their daughter used to suck the ends off lucifer matches, which could explain her death. After hearing the evidence, the jury ruled that the girl's death was accidental.

3 MARCH 1894 On this day, a woman named Susannah Dobson was brutally murdered by her lover, Richard Hodgins. The pair had been living together at a house on Fairfield Street, Chorlton-on-Medlock. On Saturday evening the couple had been drinking when they got into a physical fight. In the heat of the brawl, Dobson picked up a chair and hit Hodgins across the head. He then retaliated by hitting her with one of the chair legs, at which point Dobson fell to the ground and died. Hodgins fled to his sister's house and confessed to his crime.

At the inquest, the police surgeon noted that the hands and arms of the victim were covered in blood. He also recorded that she had a gash to her forehead, her lip was spilt and there was a puncture wound on the side of her mouth. There was also a cut behind her ear that had gone to the bone. Her chest, legs and arms were also covered in bruises.

Richard Hodgins was later tried at the Liverpool Assizes, where he was found guilty of the murder of Susannah Dobson and sentenced to death; however, after a successful petition by his solicitor and the people of Manchester, his sentence was reduced to life imprisonment.

4 MARCH 1896 Henry Norton – chief clerk of the Cheshire Lines committee – was found guilty of embezzling £4,000 of the company's money and sentenced to nine months in prison. The well-to-do gentleman was apprehended in Belgium after going

on the run and extradited back to Britain in January. Since his arrest he had complained about his treatment, stating that he objected to being chained whilst being transported to Strangeways.

Shortly after his sentence was announced, Norton made a feeble attempt to get the charge quashed, arguing that the fraud was committed because of the poorly kept books of the Cheshire Lines Company. The judge disagreed with his justification and the sentence was upheld.

A portrait of Henry Norton, who committed a daring fraud in Manchester.

5 MARCH 1901 It was on this night that a shocking murder and suicide occurred in the district of Chorlton-cum-Hardy. The victim was a respectable man named Frank Stoll Johnson, who worked as a clerk in a local solicitors. He was also a churchwarden at the local parish church and was a member of the Manchester Geographical Society.

Sometime after eleven in the evening, Johnson and his wife were in bed at their home on Keppel Street when they were awoken by the continuous ringing of their doorbell. Mr Johnson got up and went downstairs to open the door. He was greeted by a man named Nicholas Marsden, who was married to his wife's sister. In his hand was a gun. Without warning or provocation, Marsden fired several bullets into Johnson's chest. He then walked to the garden gate and turned the gun on himself. A suicide note was later found in his pocket.

Marsden, a father of two, was employed as an accountant and lived in London. His wife had been in an asylum, but was now recovering in a convalescent hospital. He had left London that morning and told his housekeeper that he was heading for Manchester. He kissed his children and informed his housekeeper that he would be back that evening.

It appears that Mrs Johnson had fallen out with her sister some years previous, although the actual motive for the murder remained a mystery. A friend of Marsden claimed at the inquest that he had been experiencing money difficulties and had spent £1,000 of his wife's money. The jury listened to the evidence and ruled that the man was insane at the time of the crime.

6   MARCH 1859   In the early hours of the morning, a fight broke out in Spinning Fields, Deansgate, which resulted in the murder of a man named William Benson and left John Warriner seriously injured. The incident occurred on the doorstep of a notorious brothel kept by Warriner.

Earlier, a shoemaker named John Mackie had turned up at the brothel to retrieve a handkerchief that he believed had been taken by a working girl named Jane Cooper. She denied taking the item and the pair began arguing, with Jane hitting Mackie over the head with a candlestick. Warriner and Cooper then kicked and beat him in the cellar. Mackie managed to escape, but returned later that night with a knife. He knocked on the door and was met by Cooper and Warriner; he then reached for his knife and stabbed Warriner in the back.

At this point Mackie walked off, but was chased by a man named William Benson. A scuffle then occurred between the pair and Mackie stabbed Benson in the abdomen and thigh, rupturing his artery. Benson died of his injuries before medical help arrived. Warriner, meanwhile, was transferred to the Royal Infirmary, where he made a full recovery.

At his trial, John Mackie was found guilty of the manslaughter of William Benson and sentenced to twelve months' hard labour.

7   MARCH 1859   A 34-year-old confectioner from Hulme, named Elizabeth Hubbert, committed suicide by throwing herself in the River Irwell. It appeared that on the previous Saturday she was due to get married, but was left at the altar. Witnesses stated that on the night in question she was seen wandering the streets, behaving strangely. Her lifeless body was discovered later that evening, face down in the river.

8   MARCH 1841   On this day, William Hampson was brought up before the borough coroner, charged with murdering Frances Bostock by cutting her throat. On the night of her death, the pair were lodging at a beerhouse on Liverpool Road owned by Henry Redford.

At some point during the afternoon, an argument occurred between the pair after Hampson told Bostock to make him some coffee, to which she refused. The pair exchanged a few words and then carried on drinking. It appears that the root of their disagreement was founded on Bostock being unwilling to continue their relationship.

At half past six in the evening, the couple were still drinking when Hampson said he was going to get some bread. He then went to the side table behind Bostock. As she was drinking, he grabbed her with one hand while he held a razor in the other. With his victim unable to escape, he then cut her throat. The wound was six inches in length and three inches deep. It had sliced through the jugular veins, exposed the larynx and the carotid artery. With blood dripping from her neck, Hampson then attempted to strangle her before fleeing the scene. Frances was attended to by people in the beerhouse before being transferred to the infirmary, where she died the following day.

The borough coroner found Hampson guilty of the wilful murder of Frances Bostock and was he sent to trial at the Liverpool Assizes. On 14 March, William Hampson was found guilty and sentenced to transportation for life.

9 MARCH 1905 A woman by the name of Sarah Sowerbutts – or Sarah Reece, as she was otherwise known – was brought up before the City Police Court charged with neglecting her illegitimate 7-year-old child. A witness stated that Sarah was employed as a shop assistant; however, her life had taken a turn for the worse after she had become addicted to drink and the company of various men. Her addiction had become so bad that she sold her daughter's petticoat for six shillings and spent the money on drink.

On 3 March, she left her child with a friend, saying that she would be back for her within the hour. However, the woman never returned and the child was found wandering the streets in a terrible state. The child appeared to be filthy and was only wearing half her clothes. The little girl was transferred to the children's home, where her underclothes were burnt. Sarah was sentenced to two months in prison.

10 MARCH 1914 An inquest was held this week into the death of 39-year-old Dr William Dowling Hamer.

On the previous Friday, Hamer's mother found him hanging from the ceiling of his bedroom. The grim discovery was made at their home on Mawson Street, Ardwick Green. At the inquest, his mother stated that there appeared to be no real motive for the man taking his own life, other than stress from studying.

11 MARCH 1838 Andrew Mulligan, 14, died after being kicked by a horse. The boy, who was employed by a local surgeon, was crossing Deansgate at the corner of Bridge Street when the horse, behind which he was running, kicked out, injuring him in the abdomen. The boy was transferred to the Royal Infirmary and later died. The post-mortem revealed that his death was caused by a ruptured bowel.

12 MARCH 1892 On this day, a man named George Jackson was sentenced to three months' hard labour for stealing a box of surgical equipment. The incident had occurred on the morning of 8 March at the surgery of Dr Conway on Newton Avenue; Jackson had called at the address and requested to see a doctor. A servant informed him that the doctor was away, but he was expected to return shortly, to which Jackson replied that he would wait in the surgery. He remained in the room for several minutes and then informed the servant that he would seek medical advice elsewhere and left. Later that evening, it was noticed that a box of medical instruments was missing and the police were called.

A few days later, Jackson took the stolen goods to a pawnshop in Macclesfield and attempted to offload the hoard. After receiving a memo from Manchester Police, the shopkeeper was already aware of the robbery and the stolen goods. The shop owner attempted to restrain Jackson, but he managed to escape. He was caught after a short chase and then handed over to the police.

13 MARCH 1830 Two brothers named Patrick and John Norton, were found guilty at the Lancaster Assizes of the manslaughter of a man named John Gready. Two months previous Gready, his wife and two children were walking along Blakely Street when they were set upon by the two brothers. Patrick Norton hit Gready on the side of the head, knocking him to the floor. John Norton, meanwhile, picked up a stone and began hitting Gready about the head. Mrs Gready pleaded with the two attackers not to kill her husband. One of the men then knocked her to the floor before they both fled. John was caught shortly afterwards, but Patrick fled to Ireland and was not apprehended for another seven weeks. The judge at the assizes sentenced both men to seven years' transportation.

14 MARCH 1870 Cab driver Thomas Walton appeared at the County Police Court charged with being intoxicated while in charge of a horse and cab. On the previous Sunday, the drunken man had been driving his cart along the Withington turnpike road when he crashed into the carriage of Mr Harvey of the Bush Hotel. Walton was found guilty and fined forty shillings.

15 MARCH 1941 This week it was reported that two police constables from Manchester and five police officers from Salford would be receiving awards for their bravery during the bombing of city during the Blitz. The Manchester constables, Henry Harper Downward and William Hanlon, received an OBE.

It was reported that Hanlon received his honour for rescuing a man from a bombed house, even though there was debris falling around him and it took him over two hours. It was stated that after his daring rescue, he remained on shift for the next forty hours. Downward received his OBE for showing skill and courage when dealing with incendiary bombs, and inspiring his colleagues during the heavy bombing of the Blitz.

16 MARCH 1875 A 54-year-old dyer named William Hall was drinking whiskey at the Bridge Inn on Beswick Street when he appeared a little worse for wear. A waiter noticed that the man was quite intoxicated and helped him outside. Once outside, the waiter placed Hall against a wall and returned to his work. A short time later, a loud thud was heard by a local shopkeeper, who ran in the direction of the noise and found Hall unconscious on the floor. He was taken to the police station where he later died and the body was then transferred to the infirmary mortuary. A post-mortem revealed that he died from a fractured skull.

17 MARCH 1874 A glazier named Michael Kilbride was found guilty of the manslaughter of 32-year-old Ellen Levell at the Subsidiary Court. The incident had occurred on 21 February, when Ellen and her sister-in-law went into the room of a man named George Hilton – who lived in the same house as Kilbride – and argued with him over some of his belongings that had gone missing.

Kilbride then suggested to Hilton that he should throw both women down the stairs, at which point Levell began attacking Kilbride, who knocked her to the floor. As she got up, she picked up a quart jug and launched it at Kilbride. For a second time he knocked Ellen to the floor and began kicking her and hitting her head against the floor. After the violent attack had finished, the men fled the scene.

Ellen Levell was admitted to the workhouse infirmary, where she remained until her death on 7 March. An inquest was held two days later, and the jury ruled that Ellen had died as a result of the fight with Kilbride and therefore he was responsible for her death.

At the trial, Kilbride was found guilty of manslaughter and sentenced to twelve months' imprisonment.

18 MARCH 1897 John Trevelyan Hutchison appeared at the Liverpool Assizes, charged with the murder of his wife and infant son. The murders occurred on 25 February at their home in Levenshulme.

The events that led to their deaths began earlier in the week, after Mr Hutchison had failed to keep up repayments to a furniture hire company, which resulted in the furniture in the living room being seized. Unable to live with the shame, Mr Hutchison wrote a suicide note and had planned to kill himself by drinking poison. Before drinking the toxic substance, he decided to murder his wife and child, because he did not want to leave them behind. He killed them both by slitting their throats from ear to ear with a razor, before placing them in bed together, as if they were asleep. The crazed man then had a change of heart and decided not to kill himself. Instead, he went to the local police station and handed himself in.

At the trial, two doctors from Strangeways prison stated that the man was not of sound mind and had irrational thoughts. The jury found Mr Hutchison guilty of the murder of his wife and child, but stated that he was not responsible for his actions. He was detained at her Her Majesty's pleasure.

19 MARCH 1858 On this day, the city coroner held an inquest into death of a poor child named Margaret Riley, who had lived with her mother at Back Charter Street. Her father was in a lunatic asylum and her mother had been reduced to begging. Mrs Riley had tried to get relief to help to her, but it had been denied. A Relief Officer did, however, visit the home and gave the girl some medicine. When he returned a few days later to check on the girl, he found the family had moved. The child was later reported to have died.

The jury ruled that the child had died from a disease of the lungs aggravated by a lack of medical care.

20 MARCH 1926 Newspapers up and down the country were reporting on the murder trial of Hector Collingwood Leach. Hector was accused of murdering his girlfriend – 18-year-old Elizabeth Haslam – in an alleged suicide pact in Southport. Leach was also charged with attempting to commit suicide.

Much to the disapproval of their parents, the young couple had been dating for over a year. On 6 March, Hector called at Elizabeth's house in Chorlton-upon-Medlock, and the pair went to a dance. On the way, Elizabeth remarked that she was 'fed up' after losing her job and did not want to return home. The dance finished at half past ten in the evening and the pair wandered in the rain, sheltering in doorways. Elizabeth tried to persuade him to go home, but Hector would not leave her. The pair decided that they would spend the night in a field and take a train to Southport the next day. After arriving in the seaside town, Elizabeth decided that she was going to take her own life. Not wanting to be parted from his sweetheart, Hector decided he would die too. The pair gathered together their change and bought a bag of sweets and a bottle of Lysol from Boots. They then returned to the promenade, where they had some tea and visited a kinema. The couple then went to the sandhills and talked, smoked and slept. At seven o'clock in the morning, the pair started to write suicide notes to their parents. After this, Elizabeth took a drink of the Lysol and dropped to the floor. Hector began hitting Elizabeth on her back to try and make her sick, but it was too late. The young man then took some of the poison himself, but he was immediately sick. He then fled to get help, but by the time the police arrived Elizabeth was already dead.

Hector Collingwood Leach was tried on 26 April 1926 at the Liverpool Assizes. After hearing all the evidence, the jury found him guilty and the judge sentenced him to death. However, he stated that he would recommend Leach to mercy on the grounds that the deceased was the brains behind the suicide pact. Hector's appeal was held on 20 May. Lord Hewart – who was conducting the proceedings – dismissed the appeal, stating that two factors made him guilty. The first was his presence at the time of the death. The second was that he bought the poison, and was therefore actually aiding and abetting the suicide. However, after hearing the verdict, the Home Secretary intervened and respited the sentence.

21 MARCH 1856 A butcher named Isaac Shaw failed to show up at the New Bailey on a charge of supplying meat that was unfit for human consumption. The Shaw family were well known to the police – Isaac's son had only just been released from prison after being convicted of three offences. The sanitary inspector of Newton Heath stated that he had collected tons of bad meat from members of the Shaw family. In his absence, the judge sentenced him to three months in prison.

22 MARCH 1870 Domestic servant Mary Jefferson appeared at the County Police Court charged with stealing some goods from her former master, Charles Keeling of Longsight. On the previous Friday, Jefferson vanished from her place of work along with a gold watch and a number of clothes belonging to Keeling's wife. The woman took the stolen items to a pawnshop on London Road and then fled to Chester. She was eventually caught with the remainder of the goods in Llandudno, found guilty and sentenced to six months in prison.

23 MARCH 1875 A most distressing murder occurred in the district of Manchester during this week. The victim was a young woman by the name of Margaret McKivett. She was killed at the hands of a quack 'surgeon' called Alfred Thomas Heap.

For over ten years, Heap had been travelling up and down the country, performing abortions. His illegal activities had resulted in him twice being arrested and once being charged for his crimes. In the late 1860s, the police finally caught up with him. He was found guilty of performing an abortion and was ordered to spend five years in penal servitude. Shortly after his release, he moved to Manchester and began practicing again, setting up his own shop in Hyde Road. His accomplice was a woman named Julia Ann Carroll, who was the landlady of the property in which he lived. Carroll would assist him in his operations and would 'look after' the girls while they were on her premises.

Hyde Road, Manchester. The scene of a horrific abortion carried out by a quack surgeon.

On 12 March, an unmarried Margaret McKivett found herself with child. Without the prospect of marriage and to avoid the stigma of having a child out of wedlock, Margaret decided to terminate her unborn baby. Desperate, Margaret began to ask around the local pubs to see if anyone knew of a doctor that could perform the procedure and spoke with a local man, who directed her to Carroll's house and told her to ask for Heap. When she arrived, she was greeted by Carroll, who informed her that the procedure would cost one sovereign. Margaret agreed and was led upstairs to the 'surgeon'.

Sensing something was wrong, Margaret's mother – who had been with her daughter in the pub – followed her to Heap's shop. Upon arriving at the door she was greeted by Carroll, who informed her that her daughter was upstairs. She then barged past the landlady and ran upstairs. In one of the rooms she found her daughter on the bed, unconscious, with the 'surgeon' trying to bring her around with something in a bottle. The mother screamed in horror, but was soon quietened by Carroll, who told her that any noise would arise suspicion from the police. As Margaret began to regain consciousness, Heap fled the house, leaving her mother to try and take the girl home. The following day Margaret was vomiting and complaining of severe pains in her abdomen. Heap was called and later arrived at the house drunk. He went upstairs and a witness heard the victim shout, 'Oh, don't!' Margaret's mother entered the room and Heap presented her with the body of the child, telling her to bury it. He also demanded two shillings and sixpence for medicine and told the girl she would not get any more unless she paid. She refused and he left. Margaret died at five o'clock the following morning. Heap was later arrested and charged with the wilful murder of Margaret McKivett.

At his trial, the jury found him guilty and he was sentenced to death by the judge.

24 MARCH 1892 A man named Richard Hodgins was charged on this day with assaulting Annie Dobson. The couple lived on Charlotte Street with Hodgins' aunt and uncle. On the day in question, he had been arguing with Dobson over two shillings and ended up giving her two black eyes. Later that day, he knocked her to the floor and she hit her head against the floor. She sustained a severe head wound and was transferred to the Royal Infirmary. Hodgins was arrested and later sentenced to three months' imprisonment with hard labour.

25 MARCH 1829 The body of a woman was found in the River Medlock near Hulme Hall. The body was transferred to the Bowling Green Inn, where it was later identified as that of Hannah Winstanley. At the inquest it was revealed that the young woman was pregnant and that she had intentionally thrown herself in the river, with the aim of ending her life. The jury returned a verdict of 'found drowned'.

26 MARCH 1913 This week a shooting accident occurred at the Old House at Home, Wilmott Street. The licensee was showing the gun to her customers when it went off and shot a 36-year-old man named William Caulder in the chest. The injured man was transferred to the Royal Infirmary, where it was hoped that he would survive.

27 MARCH 1863 Levi Taylor, 18, who resided in Shudehill, was sentenced to death for the murder of his wife, Mary Ann Taylor. Levi Taylor had grown up with his mother in Failsworth. While in Manchester, he met and fell in love with a woman of questionable character: Mary Ann. She seduced the young man and soon the pair were married. Less than an hour after the marriage, she decided to revert back to her promiscuous ways and was in the arms of another man. A few weeks later, she left her husband.

On 31 January, Levi went to visit his estranged wife, who had taken work as a servant for a beerhouse keeper. The couple went upstairs and shortly after, the victim returned with blood dripping from her throat. Levi had cut his wife's throat with a knife. Mrs Taylor attempted to speak to her landlord and then staggered into the yard. She was transferred to the infirmary, where she died of her injuries. The inquest revealed that the external and internal jugular arteries had been severed, causing her death.

At the trial it was revealed that Mary Ann had also been working in a brothel. After deliberating, the jury found Levi guilty of murder. The judge then placed his black cap on his head and passed the death sentence. The guilty man collapsed in the dock, at which point the judge stated that although Levi was guilty of murder, he was going to recommend that he man should be shown mercy. It was later reported that Levi's death sentence had been commuted to penal servitude on the grounds that his wife had provoked him.

28 MARCH 1865 The city coroner held an inquest on this day into the suspicious death of an engineer called John Parrington. On the previous Thursday evening, Parrington was walking from Market Street when a mysterious man began to follow him. As he got onto Mosley Street, he shouted at the man and the pair got into an argument. Parrington then stuck the man across the face and knocked his hat off. The man then returned a blow and knocked the engineer to the floor. He then fled the scene. Parrington died three days later. His attacker was described as wearing a light overcoat and a black hat.

29 MARCH 1894 A man called William John Read attempted to murder his 5-year-old adopted daughter Harriet O'Hara. Read and his family lived at Asquith's Court, off Oldham Road in extreme poverty. Read had been unable to find employment after he lost his job due to his failing eyesight. On the day in question, Read's wife and his 16-year-old son left the house to go to work. Later that day, their son came home to find the door locked. After a struggle, he managed to kick the door open and found his father staggering with a large cut on his neck – he had attempted suicide by cutting his throat. Read's son quickly left the house to get help, returning with a police officer. A search of the address uncovered a horrific scene – Read's adopted daughter was lying in bed with a large incision across her throat. She was transferred to the infirmary, where it was hoped that she would survive.

Read was taken to Ancoats Hospital, suffering from serious blood loss. He later died of his injuries.

30 MARCH 1894 On this day, a woman named Mary Proctor was brought up at the County Police Court charged with trying to commit suicide. Some days previous, her unconscious body had been discovered by her young daughter, slumped on the floor – she had stabbed herself with a large knife. The woman was taken to the infirmary and then transferred to the workhouse.

31   MARCH   1838   John Dixon was up in court charged with attempting to defraud the bank of Jones, Lloyd & Co.

Dixon was a member of the Hydraulic Packers' Society of Manchester. On 8 October 1837, he asked the treasurer if he could look at the books. The treasurer agreed and Dixon went off to read them. The following day he turned up at the bank and pretended to be one of the trustees of the society, with the aim of withdrawing £200. The plan worked and he left the bank with £200 in his pocket.

When the society heard of the withdrawal, it examined the bankbooks and found that the book for Jones, Lloyd & Co. had been replaced with a blank one. The bank offered an immediate reward to catch the thief: Dixon was eventually caught and taken into custody on 6 January. His trial took place on 29 March at the assizes. After listening to the evidence, the jury found him guilty and sentenced him to transportation for life.

APRIL

1 APRIL, 1911 On this day, a man named James Henry Withington was charged at the City Police Court with attempting to commit suicide. On the previous Wednesday, he wrote his wife a farewell note and then drank a bottle containing chloroform. Withington had been having money problems and was struggling to make a living. His unconscious body was discovered at a temperance hotel in the district of Strangeways. After some medical assistance, he made a full recovery.

Whilst at the Police Court, he made a promise to never try and kill himself again. He was then discharged.

2 APRIL, 1891 Two men named Patrick and John Carney broke into a shop on Medlock Street and stole thirteen pairs of boots. The pair were later caught and sentenced to six months' hard labour.

3 APRIL, 1886 A dreadful attempted murder and suicide occurred at Shakespeare Street, Ardwick. Residing at the property were Gertrude Hyman, her daughter, and a servant. Mrs Hyman, a stationer, had been separated from her husband for a number of years. At two o'clock in the afternoon, the doorbell rang and the servant answered the door to Philip Hyman, who wished to speak to his estranged wife. The servant went to get her mistress and Mr Hyman let himself into the front sitting room. Moments after Mrs Hyman went to talk to her husband, her daughter and the servant heard a scream. As their daughter entered the room, she saw her father with a gun in his hand, aiming it at her mother. He then fired a shot into the head of Mrs Hyman. Still grasping the gun, he swiftly turned around and pointed the gun at his daughter and pulled the trigger, narrowly missing her and hitting some woodwork. He then fired another shot at his wife and another at his daughter, but again he missed her. The daughter and the servant managed to escape and get help. While they had left the house, Mr Hyman placed the gun inside his mouth and pulled the trigger. He was pronounced dead at the scene. Mrs Hyman was still alive when medical help arrived, however. She had sustained two bullet wounds to her head, which were later removed, although she was left permanently paralysed following the attack.

4 APRIL, 1828 On this day, the 7th Fusiliers were residing with a Mr Parr on Cateaton Street in Manchester after travelling from Chester. The soldiers were due to leave the city on this morning and travel to Sunderland, so they were woken before seven o'clock, to ensure that they were ready for the march. At a quarter to seven, Sergeant McCartney was seen to go into the privy. Almost immediately after he entered, a shot was fired. Several men who were inside the residence rushed outside, where they found the sergeant dead, with a gunshot wound to the back of his throat. The bullet had entered through his throat and exited at the back of his head, lodging in the top of the privy. It had appeared that he had committed suicide by pulling the trigger by using his big toe – he had removed his shoe and cut a hole in his stocking. The inquest was held that afternoon and the jury concluded that the man was insane when he committed suicide.

5   APRIL 1895   On this day, the 'King of Scuttlers', Thomas Callaghan, and another scuttler named Patrick Mannion were spending their first full day in penal servitude after being found guilty of grievous bodily harm, which occurred during a show at St James's Theatre on Oxford Road. Callaghan was well known to the police and had a reputation in Manchester; the management of the theatre paid Callaghan a weekly fee to ensure that order was kept during performances. It appears that Callaghan had thrown Mannion down the gallery steps, after which he had stabbed a man named William Quinn. This then caused an affray, which resulted in several people being stabbed, although thankfully none suffered life-threatening injuries. With no previous convictions, the judge sentenced Mannion to three years' penal servitude. Callaghan had previously been convicted five times for assault and twelve times for being drunk. He was sentenced to five years' penal servitude.

6   APRIL 1923   This week a 56-year-old man named James Turner was found guilty of stealing cloth worth £40. Some days previous, two officers spotted a man wheeling a handcart, which contained the stolen fabric. The man claimed to have got the fabric from Turner and gave the police his address. The police then arrested Turner at his address on Bedford Street. At first, he denied any knowledge of the stolen fabric, but after arriving at the police station, he changed his story and admitted his guilt. He was sentenced to four months in prison.

7   APRIL 1865   Dominic Daly, 25, and 24-year-old John Barker were spending their first day in prison after being convicted of a daring robbery in Manchester. On 5 February 1865, Daly and Barker were part of a gang that broke into Mr Howard's jewellery shop on Market Street. The gang stole seven gold watches, twenty brooches, twenty gold rings, twenty gold pins and other items worth a total of £3,000. Several days after the robbery, Daly and Barker were arrested. The trial began at the sessions on 5 April and lasted for two days. Four people were tried and two were found guilty. Daly was sentenced to seven years and Barker to fourteen years.

A busy day on Market Street makes the perfect setting for a robbery.

8 APRIL, 1907 Joseph Roylance, 22, was sent to prison for nine months after being found guilty of stealing three pairs of boots.

9 APRIL, 1835 A man who called himself Thomas Brooks was brought up at the New Bailey, charged with extorting money from some of the city's American residents. The defendant claimed that he was an American. In his quest to get money, he made up a fictitious story, stating that he was from Massachusetts and had to get home but had no funds. However, his demeanour made him believable and soon he had received donations from some of his 'fellow' American migrants. Unfortunately for Brooks, one of the men he visited recognised him, as he had pulled the same stunt the previous year – the only difference was that he had stated his name as Roxburgh. Fearing that he was an imposter, one of the men called the police and he was later arrested.

After hearing all the evidence, Brooks was found guilty and sentenced to one month in prison.

A mugshot of Joseph Roylance, whose criminal career spanned more than ten years. Roylance had several distinctive tattoos dedicated to a woman named Emily. One of his tattoos was a tombstone with the words 'Emily I love you'. He also had a picture of a woman with the name Emily written underneath.

10 APRIL, 1860 A plasterer's labourer named Mr Dunn died whilst working at Victoria Station. It was his first day on the job. The young man had been assisting a plasterer who was working on some new buildings that were connected to the station. Shortly after half-past eleven, Dunn left his post to go and get some water on Cheetham Hill Road. As he crossed the track, a passing train hit him and ran over his body, severing it in several places. Dunn was pronounced dead at the scene. His body was transferred to the Manchester Arms until an inquest could be arranged.

11 APRIL, 1905 At three o'clock in the afternoon, a rag gatherer by the name of David Shields made a gruesome discovery in an unoccupied house on Hoyle Street. Shields had been gathering rags on the street when he noticed the door of No. 24 was open. After entering the property, he discovered the battered remains of a 15-year-old boy in the cellar. His mouth was stuffed with a paper and a red handkerchief was used to keep the paper in place. The makeshift gag made sure that victim was unable to shout or scream. The clothes on the boy were torn; his body was full of bruises and his middle finger nail had been ripped off, indicating signs of a struggle. Alongside the body was a bloodstained brick, which the police believed to be the murder weapon. The boy was described as about five feet in height with brown hair, grey eyes and a fresh complexion. He was later named as Thomas Smith of Wood Street. The police immediately set out to catch the killer; however, two years later, the killer was still at large and ready to strike again.

His next victim was another 15-year-old boy by the name of Stephen Kynaston, who lived with his mother at Davies Street, Ancoats. His body was also discovered in an unoccupied house on London Road, Ancoats. It appeared that the boy had been strangled, as a handkerchief was tied around his neck. The motive for both of the murders appeared to have been sexual.

A few months after the first murder, a labourer named John Leonard was arrested for acting suspiciously. It was alleged that Leonard had threatened a young lad with a razor and attempted to force him into an unoccupied house. The boy screamed and the police were called. Could this have been the working of a serial killer?

12 APRIL, 1886 A dyer named John Holland from Ancoats was charged on this day at the City Police Court with murdering his 14-month-old child. Holland had separated from his wife some months previous, but on the day in question, the pair had met up and were walking along Chester Road. Holland was carrying his child in his arms. As they reached the corner of John Dalton Street, the couple began to argue about who was to carry the child. The dyer's wife then attempted to take the baby out of her husband's arms, but Holland refused to let his wife carry the child, because she had been drinking. The woman then began to attack him with an umbrella. Holland then turned and dropped the child over a neighbouring wall, not realising that there was a twenty-foot drop. The child died instantly.

Holland was later tried and found guilty of manslaughter at the Manchester Assizes. On the grounds that he was severely provoked, the judge only sentenced him to twelve months' hard labour.

13 APRIL, 1855 On this day, two women named Mary Jones and Elizabeth Heaton were up at the City Police Court, charged with stealing. The women had taken a roll of gingham from a draper's shop in Derby Street, Cheetham. Heaton had attempted to distract the shopkeeper by looking at some stockings, while Jones took the roll of gingham, put it under her arm and left the shop. Both woman were later apprehended and sent for trial.

The trial was held on 15 June. The jury found Heaton not guilty and Jones guilty. The latter was sentenced to four months in prison.

14 APRIL, 1899 A man named Thomas Read was in the dock at the City Police Court, charged with the wilful murder of a firewood chopper named James Monks. Also in the dock was Nellie Powell, who was charged with the same offence.

The incident occurred on Friday, 4 April at a lodging house on Nelson Street, which was situated just off the Rochdale Road. It appeared that Read had accused Monks of stealing some shoes and threatened him with death if he did not return them. Shortly after, Monks entered the bathroom and was followed by Read. The pair quarrelled and then Read began hitting the man repeatedly across the head with a padlock. Monks fell to the ground and pleaded for his life, but Read just kept kicking him. Monks' son went to intervene but Read's accomplice – a woman named Nellie Powell – warned him off. She and Read then fled the scene. Help was called, but Monks died sometime later. The couple were later caught at a lodging house in Salford.

When the trial came up at the assizes, Nellie Powell was acquitted; however, Read was found guilty of wilful murder and sentenced to death. A petition was immediately set up in an attempt to have the conviction reduced on the grounds that Read was so intoxicated that he had not intentionally set out to murder Monks. The petition was successful and a reprieve was granted at the beginning of May. The sentence was reduced to penal servitude for life.

15 APRIL, 1876 A 27-year-old mechanic named William Jacques was walking home from Victoria Station when he was set upon and robbed by three men. Jacques had got as far as the junction of Hanover Street and Corporation Street when he was approached by John Lally and Thomas Wilson. The identity of the third attacker remains a mystery. As the men got close to Jacques, Lally grabbed him around the neck, while Wilson and the mystery man began to search his pockets, stealing one shilling and sixpence. The attackers then pushed him to the ground and ran off. Two of the men were later caught and arrested.

Lally and Wilson's trial was held on 11 July. After hearing the evidence, the jury found the pair guilty.

Lally was sentenced to seven years' penal servitude and seven years' police supervision. Wilson was sentenced to ten years' penal servitude and seven years' police supervision.

16 APRIL, 1891 On this day, two 18-year-old men were brought up at the Manchester City Sessions at the Sessions Court, Minshull Street, charged with unlawfully wounding a man named Anthony Gibson. On 14 February, Oswald Evison and Joseph Wood attacked Gibson with a knife. Before the evidence was heard, Evison pleaded guilty. The judge then acquitted Wood and sentenced Evison to twelve months in prison. As he was led to the cells, he shouted, 'I'll swing for you when I come out!'

17 APRIL, 1855 A woman named Ann Pearson was in the dock of the New Bailey, charged with the murder of her child. Pearson was 30 years old and lived with her parents in Chorlton-cum-Hardy.

On 27 February, she had given birth to an illegitimate son at the Chorlton Union Workhouse. After leaving the workhouse, she went to live with a lady on Silver Street, Hulme. Two weeks prior to the alleged murder, she left Silver Street, stating that she was going back to the workhouse. The events after this are somewhat unclear but it appears that she may have suffocated her son and left his body in a ditch on the road between Chorlton and Manchester. She then went to her parents' house, stating that her son had died and was now buried. Not thinking anything was amiss, the parents welcomed their daughter home.

A week later, two boys discovered the murdered child hidden in a ditch close to Redgate Farm. The little boy was wearing union clothing, a red flannel petticoat, calico petticoat and a nightcap. The child was transferred to the Horse and Jockey public house, while inquires began into the identity of the mother.

Some time later, he was identified as the young son of Ann Pearson. When questioned, she stated that her child had died in the workhouse and was buried at a churchyard in Hulme, but further investigation proved that Pearson was lying. The woman remained in custody until her trial at the next assizes.

Anne's trial was held at the South Lancashire Assizes in August. The court heard from a number of medical witnesses who could not confirm if the child had died as a result of drowning in the ditch or if he had been strangled. As there were no signs of violence on the body, the jury was left with no option other than to acquit her.

18 APRIL 1909 On this day, 39-year-old Mary Ellen Gregory was murdered at her home on Simpson Street. The victim had got into a fight with a neighbour named Mary Malone. The women were hitting each other when Malone produced a knife from her chest and stabbed Gregory. The attacker then fled the scene and ran into her house.

The Assizes Courts, Manchester.

The jury at the inquest ruled that Malone was guilty of the wilful murder of Gregory and the case was transferred for trial.

On 3 July, the case was heard at the Manchester Assizes. After listening to the evidence, the jury found Mary guilty of manslaughter. The judge sentenced her to four years in prison.

19 **APRIL 1867** A woman by the name of Jane Astell was viciously attacked with a bread knife on this day. The victim was in her home on Back Downing Street, Ancoats, when her lodger, a mechanic called Edwin Furrell, threw her on the bed and emptied her pockets. The crazed man then produced a knife and began stabbing the woman in the throat, chest and arms. Jane managed to fight off her attacker and escape outside. Furrell attempted to chase his victim but was caught by a neighbour, who kept hold of him until the police arrived. He was taken to the City Police Court, where he was remanded into custody.

20 **APRIL 1584** On this day, three men were found guilty of staying loyal to the Catholic Church by not attending Church of England services. The three men were executed and their heads were put on display at the Collegiate Church.

1870 A baker named Thomas Welsh, was found guilty at the City Police Court of stealing from his employer. The young man had stolen seven shillings from Mr Burton – a baker and flour dealer who occupied some premises on Oxford Street. While Burton was having lunch, Welsh went into the shop and stole the shillings from the money drawer. However, he was caught in the act and the police were sent for. Welsh was sent to prison for one month.

21 **APRIL 1888** On this day, the *Manchester Courier* reported on the suicide of an 18-year-old nurse named Margaret Jane Carson. She had been employed by a family that lived on Cranworth Street; however, on the previous Thursday, she was released from her position. Her master had let her go because there had been two fires in her room in the space of twelve hours. Distressed by the news, Margaret went to a chemist on Hyde Road and bought some rat poison named 'Battle's Vermin Killer'. She then left the shop, mixed the powder with a drink and then drank it. When nothing happened, Margaret went back to the chemist, claiming that the powder had gone missing. As she was handed more powder, she collapsed and died. An inquest was held the following day and it was ruled that she died by committing suicide while insane.

22 APRIL, 1905 James Callery, a 29 year old who lived on Lavender Street, died after being hit by a tramcar on Oldham Road. He was crossing the road near the Osborne Theatre when a car heading for Newton Heath hit him and dragged him along the road. Onlookers hurried over to help him. He appeared to be suffering from concussion and had a wound on the back of his head. He was transferred to the Royal Infirmary, where he died the following day.

23 APRIL, 1849 This week a man named John Fisher was apprehended for breaking into the house of a tailor and draper named Mr Bright, who lived with his family on Bradford Street. The incident had occurred on the previous Sunday. Bright left his house some time after six o'clock in the evening and went to the local chapel. Just before seven, a neighbour heard noises coming from inside the house and went to investigate. On his way, he fetched a police officer and the pair walked to the back of the property, noticed that the kitchen door had been forced open and deduced that there was someone inside the house. The two men entered the house and found Fisher upstairs rifling through the drawers. He was then taken into custody on suspicion of burglary. Fisher was well known to the police; the *Manchester Guardian* had described him as 'the most expert housebreaker in Manchester'. After being found guilty at the Borough Court, he was committed for trial at the next sessions. His trial was heard on 18 June. After hearing the evidence, the jury found him guilty and sentenced him to ten years' transportation.

24 APRIL, 1896 Two mothers named Mary Sleaford and Mary Barlow were sent to prison for neglecting their children. Barlow, who lived on Marsland Street, was found guilty of neglecting her two sons, aged 13 and 6. The two boys had been found wondering the streets in a neglected state.

Mary Sleaford, meanwhile, was sentenced to four months' hard labour for swinging her child upside down, whilst being intoxicated.

25 APRIL, 1851 On this day, a sailor named Samuel Harper was brought up at the Borough Court, charged with throwing vitriol (sulphuric acid) over a woman named Agnes Gordon. Harper and Gordon had previously been in a relationship that had ended some months prior to the incident. Since they had separated, Agnes had moved on and married another man.

It was revealed at the trial that the previous Thursday morning Harper had gone to Smithfield Market – where Gordon worked as a hawker of glass, china and second-hand clothes – and made threats against her life. He then grabbed her and attempted to pour vitriol down her throat. A scuffle broke out but she managed to fend him off. In the process of the struggle, some of the acid went over her hands and clothes, with the remainder falling on a bookstall. Gordon sustained severe burns to her hands and face and was transferred for medical help. Harper was apprehended and sent for trial.

Harper pleaded not guilty in court. He stated that Gordon's husband knocked the vitriol out of his hand when he punched him. He was then remanded to appear at the next assizes.

1870 Several newspapers reported on the inquest into the death of a young girl named Frances Jane Linney. Frances was the 6-year-old daughter of a travelling confectioner named Thomas Linney. On the day of her death, the family were working at the Knott Mill Fair. Sometime in the evening, Mrs Linney was in their caravan in Bridgewater Street when she heard screaming. Upon looking outside, she saw her daughter coming from a waggon with her clothes on fire. A man rushed over to help and the flames were put out. The girl was transferred to the Royal Infirmary suffering from burns. She died later that night.

An inquest was held the following day, in front of the coroner, Mr Herford. After hearing all the evidence, the jury concluded that the child's death was accidental.

26 APRIL, 1871 An inquest was held on this day into the death of three girls who had died at the Crumpsall Workhouse. The three girls were named as Margaret Akroyd, Sarah Ann Royle and Mary Ann Monaghan. The young ladies had been admitted to the girls' school because they had lost their parents: Monaghan was admitted because her father had deserted her and fled to America; Margaret Akroyd was admitted because her father died, and the whereabouts of the parents of Sarah Ann Royle were unknown.

On the previous Saturday, the three girls were feeling unwell and were administered 'cough medicine' by Miss Lees, who was the assistant schoolmistress. Shortly after the girls swallowed the 'medicine', they began to feel unwell. Fearing the worst, the surgeon was called and it was revealed that the girls had been given carbolic acid by mistake. Both of the bottles were similar in size and colour, but one was marked with 'poison'. All the bottles of medicine were kept with the bottles of disinfectant and Lees argued that it was an easy mistake to make.

The jury at the inquest found that the girls died by misadventure and recommended that the workhouse should not use such poisonous disinfectants in future.

27 APRIL, 1891 John Thomas Doxey, 23, appeared at the Manchester Assizes on a charge of bigamy. Doxey married a woman named Mary McLaughlin on 9 November 1890, despite already being married; he had married a Sarah Jane Ellis five

months previously, at St Barnabas church in Openshaw. Doxey admitted his guilt and was sentenced to six months' hard labour.

28 APRIL, 1850 Margaret Hannon – wife of Thomas Hannon – died on this day whilst living in filth and squalor in one of the city's slums.

Thomas Hannon was born in Ireland but left in the midst of the Potato Famine to seek a better life in Manchester. He arrived on English shores in 1847 and within a few months he had managed to secure regular work. In 1848, he had saved enough money to send for his wife Margaret and three children – who were 9, 7 and 5 years old. A year after their arrival, Thomas found himself out of work. With no income and five mouths to feed, the Hannons soon became destitute. Desperate, Thomas Hannon approached the local Poor Relief Officer, a man named Joseph Wheeler, to see if he could get any help. Sceptical of his predicament – because, according to one member of the Manchester Board of Guardians, 'the character of the Irish poor generally contained a vast amount of deception' – the Relief Officer said he would call to the house to see the conditions in which the Hannons were living.

In November 1849, Thomas and his family had moved into the cellar of No. 75 Speer Street. The cellar was spilt into two rooms – they lived in the front room and another two families (ten people in total) lived in the back room, which was eleven feet by seven feet. The room in which the Hannon family lived was ten feet square and barely tall enough for a man to stand up in. Their home contained no furniture; instead, the family slept on some old shavings, which stopped them from sleeping directly on the cold stone floor.

Shortly before the Christmas of 1849, the family were visited by the Revd Henry Browne, the priest of the Roman Catholic church on Mulberry Street. Upon seeing the desperate state of the family, the Revd Browne managed to secure some relief from two charitable funds. The occupants of both of the cellar rooms received two shillings per week, which was spilt between the three families.

The family survived until the following April on handouts from kind neighbours and local charities; however, it was not enough for them to live on. To substitute their allowance, Thomas and his children went out begging everyday. The family were in such a bad state that none of them could afford any shoes.

Margaret – who had arrived in England in good heath – soon started to deteriorate and died of pneumonia. The surgeon who examined her body commented that it was one of the most emaciated that he had ever seen.

At the inquest it was stated that although official assistance from the Poor Relief Officer would not have cured the pneumonia, it may have prolonged her life, and for this reason, Mr Wheeler was arrested and found guilty of manslaughter – a charge that was later dropped at the Liverpool Assizes.

29 APRIL, 1833 An inquest was held into the unexplained death of a porter named William Steele. He had been an excessive drinker for many years and occasionally suffered from 'fits'.

On the previous Tuesday he was feeling unwell, so his wife decided to put some leeches on his temples and let them suck out his blood. However, they had little effect and he went to bed. At some point during the night, the sick man put on his coat and hat and left the house. He was later found lying on the ground in Blackfriars Street. A passer-by helped him to his feet and he stated that he wanted to go to work at the Royal Exchange; he then grabbed the lamppost and suddenly slumped to the floor. The jury at the inquest ruled that Steele had 'died by the visitation of God'.

30 APRIL, 1895 A 60-year-old factory worker named William Thompson and Kate Goodwin, a 25-year-old servant, were tried at the Manchester Assizes on two counts of burglary. The pair had broken into a house on 6 April. They were caught in the middle of the crime, but managed to escape. Several of the stolen items were later found at Goodwin's home. The judge sentenced them both to three years' penal servitude.

At the same court, a 45-year-old hawker named Henry Bennett was found guilty of producing forged coins. On 9 March, Bennett had gone into a shop on Philip's Park Road and attempted to purchase a penny packet of cocoa. The cocoa was handed over and Bennett then produced a forged shilling. When the assistant questioned him about the authenticity of the coin, he seemed flustered and fled the shop. He was later arrested and sent for trial. He had a previous conviction for being in the possession of a mould to produce forged coins.

MAY

1 MAY 1885 A woman named Mary Walters was brought up at the City Police Court charged with assaulting her son. Mary lived with her husband and 7-year-old son John on Brunswick Street. On the day of the incident, she had sent John out to fetch her some whiskey, which she drank, hiding the bottle in one of her stockings. When her husband returned home from work, he found the bottle and confronted his wife, who flew into a rage and blamed John for telling his father where the whiskey was. The boy denied it, but his mother refused to believe him. She then picked up a red-hot poker and began hitting him with it. Once she had finished the savage attack, she sent the lad to the shop to get her more whiskey. The boy was so weak that he collapsed as he reached the shop and was transferred to the Royal Infirmary. While in hospital, the young boy was found to have severe bruising and cuts on his thighs and fingers.

After hearing the evidence, the jury found Mary guilty and she was sentenced to six months in prison with hard labour.

2 MAY 1881 This week, a brutal murder occurred in the district of Manchester. The victim was a young infant by the name of Edith Maud Watson, who was violently killed by her father Arthur Watson. Edith's parents lived in Old Trafford. They had only been married two years when Mrs Watson left Arthur because he was violent. Edith and her mother moved in with her great-uncle William Gee. On the night of Friday, 29 April, Arthur turned up at Gee's home and demanded that his wife leave with him and return to their marital home. When she refused, he stood up, grabbed a chisel and plunged it into the chest of his sleeping daughter, stabbing her four times. He then threw away the weapon and slumped into a chair. The child died almost instantly.

At a later trial, Watson was found guilty of the murder of his daughter and sentenced to death. After a petition to the Home Secretary, the sentence was reduced on the grounds that the man was insane.

3 MAY 1863 On this day, the city coroner held an inquest into the death of a child who was found wrapped in a piece of fabric in Collyhurst. The identity of the child was a mystery. A surgeon from the infirmary stated that the infant had a fractured skull, and there were marks to the neck and scalp. He went on to explain that these injuries were not self-inflicted. The jury listened to the evidence and found that the child had been murdered, but the culprit was unknown.

4 MAY 1929 The police were called to a hosiery shop on Grange Terrace, Rusholme. The owner of the premises was 72-year-old George Armstrong. Members of the public and the police had become concerned for his welfare after he failed to open his shop.

Broadmoor Criminal Lunatic Asylum, 1867.

After arriving at the scene, a police officer managed to force the door open and get inside. Upon reaching the stairs, he noticed the lifeless body of Mr Armstrong lying in a pool of blood. He had ten incision wounds to the face and head and what appeared to be a fractured jaw. The police immediately launched a murder investigation. The motive for the crime appeared to have been a robbery: Armstrong's pockets were turned inside out, the takings were missing and there were empty hatboxes.

The police appealed for several men to come forward and rule themselves out of the enquiry. Eventually they arrested a 30-year-old man named George Fratson, who resided in Royton. He was arrested after he made several statements admitting to the crime. He was found guilty and sentenced at the assizes on 9 July. At the trial he withdrew all of his statements and began to claim that he was innocent. However, the jury disagreed and ruled that the man was guilty. The judge then sentenced him to death. The authorities later rejected two appeals made by Fratson against his 'guilty' verdict. However, his death sentence was reduced to penal servitude and he was transferred to Broadmoor Criminal Lunatic Asylum.

5 MAY 1847 A brutal murder occurred on this day in the district of Chorlton. The victim was a market gardener by the name of Francis Dakin, who was violently stabbed to death whilst drinking in a beerhouse. Dakin was a married man with six children, the youngest being only 3 years old at the time of his death.

Dakin had arrived at the beerhouse – situated across the road from his house – sometime before nine o'clock in the morning. The house was owned a lady called Mrs Leach. Her estranged husband, George Leach, was also drinking in the premises. It appeared that about four o'clock in the afternoon, an argument broke out between Mr and Mrs Leach, which ended in Mr Leach calling his wife a whore. Dakin witnessed the incident and confronted the husband, telling him to not speak to his wife in that manner. A witness then reported that an argument broke out between the pair, which resulted with Leach leaving the room and returning with a carving knife. Without warning, George Leach lunged at Dakin, stabbing him in the right breast. The seven and a half-inch blade was driven into the chest with such force that it cut straight through the windpipe. Dakin immediately fell to the floor and died almost instantly. The inquest was held a day later at the Horse and Jockey in Chorlton. The jury returned a verdict of wilful murder and Leach was sent for trial.

His trial was held on 11 August at the Liverpool Assizes. After hearing the evidence the jury found him guilty of manslaughter and he was sentenced to transportation for life.

6   MAY   1893   Thomas Matthews, 27, was sitting on the doorstep of a house in Nicholas Street, Angel Meadow, when, without warning, a man called Henry Burgess walked past and threw a lit oil lamp at him. The lamp smashed on Matthews, setting fire to his clothes. Some people who were walking past ran over and attempted to put out the flames, but it was too late. Matthews was so severely burnt that he died later of his injuries. Burgess was apprehended to stand trial at the Police Court on the following Monday.

7   MAY   1863   An inquest was held into the death of Jane Smith, who had allegedly died after her husband John Smith had hit her on the head with a poker. The couple had been arguing when Mrs Smith picked up a poker and attempted to attack her husband with it. Mr Smith then wrestled with his wife and pulled the poker out of her hand; he then hit her across the head with it, causing her to lose her balance and fall down the cellar steps. After hearing the evidence, the jury ruled that John Smith was guilty of manslaughter and he was committed for trial.

His case was heard at the South Lancashire Assizes in August. After listening to the evidence, the judge found him guilty of the manslaughter of his wife. He was sentenced to eighteen months in prison.

8   MAY   1900   Ann Birtles, who lived on Marsland Street, Ardwick, was savagely murdered by her husband John.

The Birtles had two sons: the youngest slept through the incident and the eldest was at work when his mother was killed. It appeared that sometime before eleven o'clock in the evening, Ann was carrying some water into the kitchen when for no reason other than being under the influence of alcohol, Mr Birtles began attacking his wife with a crowbar. Bruises on Ann's arm suggested that she had tried to block the blows. However, her husband was hitting her with such force that he broke both jaws and her right cheekbone. She also suffered a fracture to her skull that stretched from her eye, over the forehead and to the other eye as well as a second fracture, starting on her forehead and extending to the back of the head. The cause of death was a haemorrhage on the brain, which had resulted from the fractures.

The police were called by the eldest son, who had stumbled upon the gruesome scene after returning home from work. Mr Birtles confessed to the killing and was sent to the next assizes for trial. His trial was held on 17 July at the Manchester Assizes. After hearing the evidence, the jury found him guilty and the judge sentenced him to death. However, he was later spared the death penalty on the grounds that he was insane and was instead transferred to Broadmoor Criminal Lunatic Asylum where he would remain at Her Majesty's pleasure.

9   MAY 1875   On this day, four pickpockets were awaiting trial in a Manchester prison. Their names were James O'Canavan, James Myers, John Ackland and John Vine. All four men were apprehended in Manchester and charged with intending to commit a felony.

Later that month Ackland, Vine and Myers were found guilty and sentenced to three months in prison. O'Canavan was wanted on a separate charge and was committed to the sessions accused of being an incorrigible rogue and a vagabond. He was sentenced to ten months in prison.

John Ackland.   James O'Canavan.   John Vine.   James Myers.

10 MAY **1892** Several national newspapers reported on the death of a prominent Birmingham jeweller named Michael Joseph Goldschmidt, who had left Birmingham on Monday morning to do business. After catching a train from Liverpool, he arrived in Manchester on Thursday afternoon. At the station he employed a porter to transport his goods to various clients. Goldschmidt had brought with him £2,000 worth of jewellery samples – roughly £215,000 in today's money. His first stop was a jeweller on Deansgate named Mr Steel. Goldschmidt left the porter outside with the cases and went inside. Whilst he was conducting his business, the porter became distracted and started looking in a shop window. Moments later he turned around and found that one of the bags had gone missing from the handcart. He immediately called Goldschmidt and a search for the stolen bag began.

After reporting the crime, Goldschmidt went to a chemist on Deansgate and bought a bottle of cyanide potassium. At first the pharmacist refused to sell him the poison. He was only allowed to buy it after a witness verified that the man was a jeweller and that the product would only be used to clean jewellery. Goldschmidt then went back to the Spread Eagle Hotel on Corporation Street. The following morning, he did not leave his room. Worried for Goldschmidt's safety, an attendant and a police officer forced open the door and found the jeweller dead. In a glass next to the body was a small quantity of the poison. The man had committed suicide.

The crime remained unsolved for the next two years. However, on 1 August 1894, a dealer named George Jones was found guilty of the robbery and sentenced to eighteen months in prison.

11 MAY **1851** On this day, three girls appeared at the Borough Court charged with intimidating workers at the George Woolley & Son mill on Ancoats Street. On the previous Wednesday, a large majority of Woolley Mill's workforce were on strike. Amongst those protesting outside the mill were Elizabeth Desour, Margaret McAvety and Mary Ann Milligan. Like a scene out of Elizabeth Gaskell's *North and South*, the mill owner had employed strike-breakers.

As the new workforce was heading into the mill, they were threatened and verbally abused. Some of the angry mob threw stones at the operatives. Such was the menace of the crowd that one woman fled and hid in a nearby shop and another refused to go back to work.

The judge found all three women guilty of intimidation and sentenced them to hard labour for seven days. Although he sympathised with their cause, he stated that the victims had the same right to work as the prisoners and that if they were caught again, they would face a much tougher sentence.

12 MAY 1828 The body of a widow named Mary Eastwood was discovered on the corner of Garratt Bridge. The woman was only partially clothed and there was evidence to suggest that she may have been sexually assaulted. Suspicion immediately fell on a man named Elijah Mayers, who had been living with Mary. On the night in question the pair had been drinking at the Union Tavern, which was only a few yards from Garratt Bridge. The pair left the pub together and appeared intoxicated.

After the discovery of the body was made, Mayers was arrested and charged with murder. At the inquest, a doctor claimed that the woman had died as a result of a fit. The jury agreed and released Mayers. The public were outraged and disgusted by the result. Such was their hostility that Mayers had to be transported to the Town Hall by coach. Hostile crowds also gathered outside his home at Bank Top.

13 MAY 1909 The body of a young woman was found in a field near the Gorton sewage works. The victim was named as 27-year-old Emily Ramsbottom. A post-mortem revealed that she had died from strangulation. The prime suspect was an ex-lover named Mark Shawcross.

At the inquest, the sister of the victim stated that on the night of her murder, Emily had left the house with Shawcross. Fearing for her sister's safety – Shawcross had a reputation for violence and he had hit Ramsbottom in the past – the girl decided to follow the pair. After a short while, the girl returned home. The next time Emily was seen was at half past five the next morning, when a man walking to work discovered her body. A hunt was launched for Shawcross, but he had gone on the run.

For seven days he goaded the police, sending them letters where he admitted to the murder and threatened other members of the public. He was eventually tracked down a week later and charged with the woman's murder. On 6 July, Mark Shawcross was found guilty of the murder of Emily Ramsbottom and sentenced to death. He was executed on the morning of 2 August at Strangeways prison. Emily left behind three children from a previous marriage.

14 MAY 1852 On this day, an elderly woman by the name of Mary Ormes committed suicide by drinking a bottle of vitriol. The deceased had separated from her husband and was living on Allan Street. On the previous evening – in an intoxicated state – she went to the druggist and purchased three pennies worth of vitriol, telling him it was to be used to clean clothes. After purchasing the acid, she then walked to her husband's house on Lancashire Street, Hulme. Upon reaching the house, she sat on the step and swallowed the vitriol. She was found shortly after and taken inside her husband's house. The surgeon was sent for and battled in vain to make the woman sick. Mary Ormes died the following morning.

15 MAY 1925 Several newspapers reported that a married man named James Makin was to be remanded in custody on a charge of murdering Sarah Ann Clutton. The murder had occurred on 4 May at the home of James Makin and his wife.

Makin had spent the day drinking with Sarah, when they decided to go back to his house on Cross Street, Newton Heath. The pair got into a quarrel and, without warning, Makin picked up a knife and began stabbing her in the throat. Sarah died instantly. Makin went back to the pub before handing himself in. The body of the woman was later discovered by his wife slumped on the bedroom floor. The couple had only been married since January.

James Makin was later found guilty of Sarah's murder. He was executed at Strangeways on 11 August.

16 MAY 1862 Shortly after half past eight on this morning, an estate agent named Evan Mellor left his home in Old Trafford and headed to his office on South King Street. Mellor and his son operated out of an office in St James's Chambers. He arrived shortly after nine o'clock and made his way up the stairs to the second floor. As he approached his office door, he was met by William Robert Taylor and Martha Ann Taylor, who

were man and wife. William was holding a large knife and his wife was armed with a gun. Without warning, William launched at Mellor, repeatedly stabbing him in the chest. The wounded man managed to stagger downstairs and get the attention of a porter. The porter attempted to shield Mellor, but was shot in the arm by the attackers. The couple then fled.

Evan Mellor died at the scene and the porter was transferred to the Royal Infirmary. The attackers were eventually caught and sent to the police station at the Town Hall. While there, William Taylor gave the officer a key and told him to go to his home at Britannia Buildings, Strangeways.

The officers arrived at the upmarket shop and found the key opened a back bedroom. Once inside, the officers made a horrific discovery: lying on the bedroom floor were Taylor's three children. The children were dressed in long white nightdresses, with black bands around their wrists, and each had a label with their name and age placed upon their chest – Mary Hannah Taylor, 11 years old; Hannah Maria Taylor, 6 years old and William Robert Taylor, 4 years old. The bodies also contained a note denouncing Mellor and Son as 'murderers'. The appearance of the children was immaculate; their hair had been brushed and their bodies had been arranged with the utmost of care. As there was no sign of any physical violence, the officers concluded that they had died from some kind of poisoning.

Further investigation revealed that sometime in October, Taylor had rented a shop from Mellor for approximately £50 per annum. The following month, Taylor approached Mellor about fixing a broken boiler that was in danger of bursting. Mellor took no action, and during a period of cold weather, the boiler froze and then burst, killing one of Taylor's daughters. Shortly after this time, it appeared that Taylor got into financial difficulty. Neighbours reported bailiffs coming to the house and removing all the furniture – they even took a comb from the hand of his daughter while she was combing her hair.

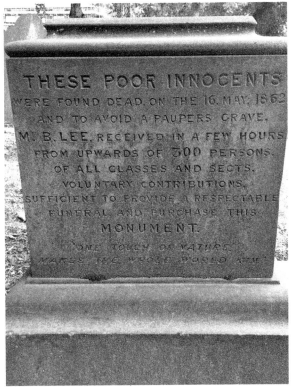

William Robert Taylor and Martha Ann Taylor were subsequently charged with murder and committed for trial at the assizes. Martha was acquitted. William was found guilty and sentenced to death for the murder of Mellor and his three children. He was executed on 13 September at Lancaster Castle. The execution attracted a large crowd – one of the papers reported 100,000 – who had come from Liverpool, Ashton, Manchester and other areas. On the morning of his final day on this earth, he wrote a letter to his wife and his sister. In his pocket he had a handkerchief that he had promised to get sent to his wife after his death.

His execution took place shortly before twelve o'clock in the afternoon. His body remained hanging for an hour before being taken down. A cast was then made of his head and his body buried within the prison.

17 MAY 1911 Over the previous week, three instances of cycle theft had been heard at the sessions. All the bicycles had been left outside buildings in the city. The first thief was sent to prison for twelve months. The second thief was a man named William Yarwood, who worked as a clerk. He was found guilty of stealing two cycles and selling them on for a small sum of money. A servant named Louie Mardsen was sentenced to three months in prison for buying a bicycle, knowing it was stolen.

18 MAY 1869 Fifteen men were brought up at the City Police Court, charged with allowing betting on their premises. The operation to close down illegal betting establishments was brought about by the local police.

The first man to stand in front of the magistrate was Thomas Forshaw, who lived on Milk Street. Forshaw admitted to taking bets in a converted office, which was inside his home. Inside the office was a desk, which contained betting lists and racing cards. The next defendant was a man named Joseph Crossley, who kept the Vine Inn beerhouse on Thomas Street. Crossley was caught after an undercover officer went in and made a bet on two occasions. The undercover officer also witnessed several other people betting on horses.

After hearing all the evidence, the magistrate discharged one of the men and found the other fourteen guilty. Two of the men were given the full £100 fine, as they had been caught before. The rest were fined the heavy sum of £75. Failure to pay the fine would result in a three-month stay in prison.

19 MAY 1927 On this day, 43-year-old John Douglas Rodda was found dead in his office on Deansgate. Rodda worked as an agent and his family home was on Meadow Street, Moss Side. He had five children and for the past four years he had been bringing them up on his own after he had separated from his wife. A lady named Mrs Day found Rodda with his head near the gas fire and a note by his side. It appeared that the man had committed suicide by gassing himself. A witness stated that she believed that the man had killed himself because he was worried about the financial state of his business.

The inquest was held on the following day in Manchester. The coroner ruled that Rodda died from suicide while insane.

20 MAY 1900 A 53-year-old actor named George Sennett was today found dead in his room at Cumberland Street, Deansgate. The coroner ruled that the man possibly committed suicide from laudanum poisoning and alcohol.

21 MAY 1851 An inquest was held at the Wheat Sheaf public house, Lloyd Street. The victim was a 3-year-old child named Maria Steele. She was the daughter of a bricklayer named George, who resided at 7 Cross Street, Hulme. On the previous Sunday, Maria had been left in the care of her elder brother. At some point in the morning, the brother left the house to nip across the street. Upon returning, he found his sister engulfed in flames. He managed to put out the fire, but she had suffered severe burns and died five days later. The jury ruled that the young girl's death was an accident.

22 MAY 1888 On this day an inmate at Stangeways prison murdered prison warder Ralph Dyer Webb. Webb was born in Cheltenham in 1843. Some time later, he moved to Salford and married a local girl called Grace Barlow. The couple lived on Cotham Street and had two children, Eliza and Ralph Jnr.

The tragic events occurred in the matron's house, which was situated within the grounds of the prison. Webb was in the matron's house to watch over a prisoner called John Jackson, who was fixing a leak. Jackson was serving six months in prison because he had been found guilty of committing a number of robberies. It appeared that Jackson had started to fix the leak when he saw an opportunity to overcome the warder and escape. It is unclear exactly what happened, but what is known is that Jackson picked up a hammer and hit Webb several times on the back of the head, fracturing his skull and knocking him to the floor. While Webb lay dying, Jackson emptied his pockets and stole his boots. He was only interrupted when he heard the matron knock at the door. Unable to get inside – the door was locked from the inside – the matron called for help, but by the time Webb was found, Jackson had escaped through a hole in the roof. Two boys confirmed that they saw the murderer come through the roof and escape down Southall Street. They stated that when he saw them, he threatened to kill them if they shouted or approached him.

Jackson was now on the run. He managed to evade capture for over two months, finally being caught in Bradford on 11 June. He was apprehended after he broke into a house on the Leeds Road, where the owner managed to restrain him until the police arrived. Once he was identified, he was then swiftly taken back to Manchester, where it was revealed that his real name was Charles Wood Firth. At the County Police Court he was charged with breaking into the house of Marshall Booth in Bradford and also the murder of the warder, Webb. He was later sentenced to death.

The night before his execution, Jackson went to sleep at ten o'clock but only managed to get a couple of hours' rest. He awoke at six o'clock and had a breakfast of buttered bread and a cup of tea. The chaplain then went to see him and the pair prayed. A little before eight o'clock the executioner entered the room, shook hands with Jackson and said goodbye. He then carried out his duty. Jackson died quickly. His body was left hanging for an hour.

23 MAY 1854 A woman named Harriet Ann Turner was brought up at the City Police Court, charged with stealing a child. The child was the 6-month-old daughter of a widower named Patrick Henry. According to Henry, Turner turned up at his lodging house on Garden Street, looking for a place to stay. He agreed that she could stay rent-free, as long as she looked after his daughter.

Turner continued to lodge at the house and look after the girl until 7 April. On that day, she left with the infant, saying she was going to get some medical advice, but she did not return. Instead she took the child and fled to Liverpool. On 16 April she was admitted to the Liverpool Workhouse, along with Henry's daughter, who died later that day. Turner stayed in the workhouse until 1 May. From Liverpool she went to Macclesfield and remained there until she was apprehended and handed to the police. The woman was then transferred back to Manchester to face trial at the next sessions.

On 16 June 1854, she was found guilty of stealing a child and sentenced to twelve months in prison.

24 MAY 1889 A post-mortem was held on the body of John Bacon, who died at Victoria Station. The man entered the station and was hit by a train. The train ran over his legs and completely severed them from his body. He was transferred to the Royal Infirmary, where he died the following day from his injuries.

25 MAY 1833 On this day, four German men were preparing to commit a robbery at the home of Martin Schunck, who was a partner in the company Schunck, Mylius & Co. The robbery was only rumbled after one of the men reported the plan to the police. As soon as the police got wind of the planned attack, they sent two officers to the address on Moss Lane, Rusholme. The officers told Schunck of the proposed robbery and set a trap for the burglars: they lowered all the blinds and blew out the candles so the thieves would think that the family was asleep. The officers also removed the family dogs so they could hear the burglars when they arrived. The two officers then positioned themselves in the pantry. They were armed with batons, a gun and a lantern. Schunck and a man named Philip Merz – his son's tutor – positioned

Lancaster Castle, the home of some of Manchester's most notorious criminals.

themselves upstairs so they could see the front of the house. Shortly after one o'clock in the morning, Merz and Schunck observed a man trying to gain entry to the house through a window in Mrs Schunk's room. The men went and told the officers and all the men proceeded to confront the robbers.

The officers opened the front door and caught two men up a ladder trying to break into the house and another fleeing the scene. One of the officers immediately pushed the ladder over and fought with the robbers, but one managed to escape. All the men were later seized in the vicinity of the property.

It was later revealed at the trial that some of the robbers were from well-respected German families. Schunck knew one of the men personally. It appeared that he had been kind to the man and offered him financial relief. This man had been inside Schunck's house and knew it contained valuables.

The jury found all three men guilty of burglary and sentenced two of them to two years' hard labour, while the other man was imprisoned for twelve months with hard labour. All of them would serve their sentence at Lancaster Castle.

26 MAY 1875 An inquest was performed on the body of a woman who had been found floating in a pond off Queen's Road. The identity of the woman was a mystery, but she was roughly 55 years old and wearing a red French bodice, white cotton stockings, white cotton skirt and two odd boots. The jury ruled that she died from drowning.

27 MAY 1847 Early on this morning, a man named Thomas Royle and his wife were fast asleep in his mother-in-law's home. She was an elderly lady named Elizabeth Jackson and lived in a small property on Crator Street, Hulme. The house contained only one bed, so on the night in question, Jackson, Royle and his wife were all sharing.

Sometime in the early hours, Elizabeth Jackson awoke and reached over her daughter to grab a large table knife. Then, without warning, she slit the throat of her son-in-law. Luckily the knife was blunt, although it did not stop him receiving several serious wounds to his throat and hands. Royle eventually managed to fend off his mother-in-law and escape to the house next door.

Jackson was later apprehended and sent to the Liverpool Assizes on a charge of attempted murder.

28 MAY 1884 Sixteen-year-old Elizabeth Donnelly died from stab wounds in the Manchester Royal Infirmary on this day. The victim lived with her family at George Leigh Street, Ancoats.

The incident had occurred two nights previous, when Elizabeth and her 27-year-old brother Joseph James Donnelly got into an argument over a glass of water. Joseph and Elizabeth were both upstairs when he decided that he wanted a drink. Rather than go himself, he demanded that his sister went downstairs in her nightdress to get him one. When she refused, Joseph left the room and returned with a razor. He then grabbed his sister by the waist and began savagely attacking her, causing several cuts to her body and a serious cut to her throat.

On hearing the commotion, the children's mother attempted to intervene, but the crazed son then turned his attention on her and began a similar assault. He then fled the room and hid on the roof behind some chimneys.

Elizabeth died two days later. She had suffered a two-foot wound stretching from her thigh and across her abdomen, as well as other serious injuries. Joseph was later arrested and tried at the assizes. His defence tried to claim that he had murdered his sister and attempted to murder his mother while he was having a fit. The jury took forty-five minutes to find him guilty of murder and the judge then passed the death sentence.

After a visit from a medical officer from Broadmoor Criminal Lunatic Asylum, the Home Office ordered that the sentence of death should be reduced to life in prison at Her Majesty's pleasure.

29 MAY 1849 On this day, two thieves who were known as 'Forty Fox' (John Fox) and 'Apple Daddy' (Thomas Vernon) were charged at the Borough Court with stealing six sovereigns, a quantity of silver, a silver snuffbox and a watch from an old man on Market Street. Their accomplice was a woman named Esther Hill, who convinced the old man to walk her home. As the pair got to Market Street, the old man was knocked to the floor by Vernon and Fox and robbed. The old man handed Hill the snuffbox and the three made their escape. All three were transferred from the Borough Court and were sent for trial at the next assizes.

30 MAY 1856 At eight o'clock in the evening, a well-dressed, mysterious man walked into the tobacconist shop in Chapel Street and asked the owner's wife the price of a cigar case. The woman gave him the price and he handed her a sovereign. Unsure of the authenticity of the coin, the woman left the man in the shop while she showed the coin to a servant. While she was out of the room, he began helping himself to the contents of the till. The shopkeeper's daughter – who was also in the room – caught the man in the act and began shouting to her mother, who rushed in, but it was too late: the man had gone. Two cap-makers who were working downstairs heard the commotion and attempted to chase the man, but he fled into the night with over £70 in coins and notes.

31 MAY 1892 A young scuttler named William Willan should have been executed today for the murder of Peter Kennedy. Willan, Edward Fleming and Charles Davidson – who were all 16 years of age – were tried at the Manchester Assizes on 20 May for wilful murder.

The incident had occurred on 8 May on the corner of Alum Street. Willan, Fleming and Davidson were part of the 'Lima Street Gang' and were known to have disagreements with other rival gangs in the area, such as the Bradford Street Gang, of which Kennedy was a member.

On the day of the murder, the three lads were armed and ready for a fight. Willan had a knife and the other two lads had a belt and a stick. The gang took up their positions on Great Ancoats Street and waited for Kennedy to appear. When their target was in sight, Willan crept up behind him and repeatedly stabbed him in the back. All the lads then fled the scene.

When the trial was heard at the assizes, Fleming and Davidson were acquitted, but Willan was found guilty and sentenced to death. His execution was due to take place on 31 May; however, it was postponed while a petition was sent to the Home Secretary. On account of the boy's age, the sentence was later commuted to penal servitude for life.

JUNE

1   JUNE   1830   At nine o'clock in the morning, an agitated young woman rushed past a former police officer named Mr Derbyshire, and another man named Mr Clifford, heading for the banks of the River Irwell. Fearing something was wrong, the men followed her along the path. As she got near the bank, she attempted to jump in but was saved by the men, who managed to grab her. However, the woman struggled, managed to break free and plunged into the water. The men dived in after her and rescued her by dragging her to the shore.

2   JUNE   1875   On this day, the deputy coroner of the city held an inquest into the mysterious death of a 21-year-old bricklayer named Thomas Neal. The man lived with his wife, Elizabeth, on Cowcill Street, Hulme.

On 23 May, Neal began feeling ill and spent the whole of that night vomiting violently. The following morning he was unable to talk, so his wife sent for medical assistance. The doctor prescribed some medicine, which Neal took with some brandy. Later that day his condition worsened and he was admitted to the infirmary suffering from symptoms similar to laryngitis. Neal succumbed to his illness the following day.

A doctor at the infirmary carried out a post-mortem on the body, but could find no evident cause of death, although he did notice a mark on the man's arm, which appeared to be from an animal bite. A friend of the deceased confirmed that the victim did use to own a retriever. The friend also stated that Neal had told him that a dog had bitten him twelve months ago while in Withington.

The jury returned a verdict that the man had died from hydrophobia (rabies).

3   JUNE   1846   On this day, racegoers gathered at the Manchester Races for the Wednesday meet. Riding one of the horses was a gentleman from Dublin called James Melvin Byrne, who had left Ireland shortly before his marriage to Elizabeth Pellew in 1841. Pellew was the only daughter of the very wealthy Major William Anthony Bale of Ashford, Shropshire. After the couple wed, they moved to a cottage near Tenbury, Worcestershire.

Byrne was no stranger to racing; he was regarded as an experienced and competent steeplechase rider. He arrived in Manchester shortly before the race and took up residence at the Post Office Hotel. On the day of the race, Byrne was riding in the steeplechase on a horse called Rhoderick. The first race started just after two o'clock in the afternoon. There were two false starts before the horses finally set off. At the start of the race, Byrne's horse was leading followed by a horse called The Doe. All the horses safely made it over the first hurdle. As they got to the second hurdle, Bryne jumped clear, but another horse called Alice which was jumping at the same time hit his horse on the shoulder, causing him and another horse to fall on the track. The jockey of the other horse managed to escape but Byrne was seriously injured. He was transferred to the Royal Infirmary, where he died the following day of head injuries.

4 JUNE 1877 John Hamin and Elizabeth Stewart were sent to prison for three months' hard labour after being found guilty of attempting to pickpocket at Victoria Station. Ellen Sullivan and William Mason were also charged with the same crime and they were sentenced to two months' hard labour.

A depiction of Hamin and Stewart awaiting trial.

5 JUNE 1906 A man named James Roberts was on trial for assaulting a woman named Mary Connolly with a knife in an attack at a lodging house in Addington Street. Connolly and Roberts had lived together for a year, but had recently separated.

On the night in question Connolly was enjoying the company of a friend when Roberts burst into the room and began attacking her with a knife. She received two wounds to the head and was transferred to the Royal Infirmary, where she made a full recovery.

After listening to the evidence, Roberts was found guilty and sentenced to two months in prison.

6 JUNE 1887 A bolt-maker named James Dodd and his partner Harriet Turner were at their home on Back Hadfield Street. Dodd lived at the house with his two daughters and three sons. The property was on one level and comprised of two rooms – a room to eat and a bedroom.

Dodd had been living with Turner since the death of his wife. Turner was a widow herself – she had been married to an engineer in St Helen's called Charles Seymour, but he had since died.

Some time the following day, the couple decided to go out drinking. They returned home shortly after six o'clock and appeared to be intoxicated. The couple went to bed arguing, and in the early hours of the morning, Dodd's son awoke to find his father bent over Turner, who appeared to be struggling to get free by kicking her legs. He had a razor in his hand and was slitting her throat, while pushing her head back into the pillow. Blood was gushing from her neck, nose and mouth, and her head was almost severed from the body. After the act had been committed, Dodd sat back and calmly took a drink of water. He then wiped the razor and placed it back into his pocket. With a sudden sense of urgency he then fled downstairs into the street, shouting to his son that he would never see him again. The son tried to give chase to his father but returned to the house after Dodd threatened to slit his throat with the razor unless he left him.

The following day, a boatman who lived in Hulme was travelling along the Rochdale Canal when he noticed a body under the Union Street Bridge. The body was recovered and identified as James Dodd, who had committed suicide by jumping from the Union Bridge, after murdering Harriet Turner.

7 JUNE 1913 On this day, a woman's body was found on Western Street in Ardwick. The victim was a young married woman named Daisy Clarke. She died after her throat was cut with a knife. The attacker was later identified as her estranged husband, Robert Clarke. Unable to live with the guilt, he handed himself in after he had committed the atrocious crime. He was remanded in custody until his trial.

8 JUNE 1885 This week Manchester was coming to terms with the shocking double murder of two young children. James, aged 5, and John, 3, were the only children of John and Margaret Hibbert. The Hibberts were a wealthy middle-class family, who employed two servants and lived in a large seven-roomed house in the leafy suburb of Moss Side.

On the morning of Friday, 5 June, Mrs Hibbert asked one of the servants to send the children upstairs so she could give them a bath. She then told the servant to go to the shop to fetch some soda water. While she was out of the house, Mrs Hibbert took her youngest son into the bathroom and held him down in the bath until he drowned, before covering the body in a blanket and laying it out on the child's bed. After leaving the bedroom, she called the eldest son upstairs and repeated the heinous crime. Once both children were on the bed, she wrote a jumbled suicide note to her father, stating how she was not going to heaven. Margaret then attempted to commit suicide by drowning herself in the bath, but was stopped by the servant and a neighbour.

It appears that Mrs Hibbert had been plagued with mental health problems since the birth of her child thirteen months previous. Worried for her safety, her husband committed her to an asylum from which – against the advice of medical professionals – she was later released. It was discovered that Margaret's husband signed her out, stating that he would take special care of her. After the death of her children, she refused to believe that they were dead, stating that they could not die. At the inquest, the coroner passed a verdict of wilful murder.

9   JUNE 1888   A fire broke out at a stationer's shop occupied by Martha Gains and her son, which was situated on the corner of St Andrew's Street and Fairfield Street. Above the shop were two flats, in which four people were asleep.

Shortly after eleven o'clock in the evening, Martha's son, Daniel, heard a loud knock at the front door. He went downstairs and discovered a fire in the kitchen. He managed to escape and called for the fire brigade. Assuming that all occupants of the house had escaped, he then went to a neighbour's house to recover. A fireman arrived on the scene within three minutes of being called.

A crowd that had gathered outside the burning building informed the fireman that all the occupants had escaped. The man then began to tackle the fire on his own until back-up arrived from the Manchester Fire Brigade. By the time of their arrival, however, the fireman had since learned that Mrs Gains was in fact still inside the building. Firemen Hunt and Wright managed to get into the room where she had been sleeping and discovered the badly burned bodies of Mrs Gains and her 17-year-old servant Mary Owen. The men removed the women and went back to search the property. In another room they found 14-year-old Tomas Owen (brother of the servant) and Charles Clegg, who had both been employed at newspaper sellers. The two boys were alive when they left the property and were transferred to the infirmary. One of the boys died on the way and the other died after reaching the infirmary.

10   JUNE 1829   The 10-year-old son of Mrs Westerman was found dead in the Rochdale Canal at Greythorn. The young boy had been bathing when he got into difficulty and drowned. His body was not discovered until the following evening.

Mrs Westerman lived on George Street and had been struggling to raise her ten children since the death of her husband. Upon hearing of her son's death, she was called to identify the body, but it appears that the trauma of seeing her dead son was too much for her. The following morning, her children were unable to wake her from her sleep and Mrs Westerman was pronounced dead at the scene.

11 **JUNE 1887** On this night, a terrible accident occurred at a shoe factory in Hulme. The factory was owned by John Reavy and was situated at 76 and 78 River Street.

Reavy had moved into 78 River Street with his wife, Eliza, in the late 1870s. In the early days of his shoe business, he owned just one shop, employing four workers. By the time of the accident, the business had grown and Reavy had expanded his business, with the purchase of a second shop, employing eleven workers.

On the night in question, Reavy and his staff were working when they heard a loud noise. Fearing something was wrong, he quickly ushered everyone into the street. After waiting for a few minutes, a group of workers and some of the customers returned to the shop. Reavy and the other workers waited in the street.

As soon as the group returned to the shop, a large crack was heard and those stood outside shouted for everyone to immediately leave the building. Nearly everyone had escaped when the central part of the factory collapsed, trapping the remainder of the people in the debris. The fire department arrived a short time later and began rescuing the victims. Five people were brought out alive and, some time in the early hours, the firemen discovered the bodies of two females. The first woman was named as 33-year-old Ann Jane McDonough of Claro Street, Hulme. The second victim was identified as 58-year-old Mrs Cheetham, who lived at the Young Ladies' Christian Association in Dukinfield.

12 **JUNE 1890** Elizabeth Turner – who also went by the aliases Margaret Black, Margaret Graham, Margaret Rogers, Margaret James, Margaret Rylance or Theresa Mack – was found guilty of stealing a dress and sentenced to fifteen months in prison.

Between 1886 and 1906, Elizabeth had obtained twenty-four convictions for stealing. Her crime spree spread across the north-west: she had stolen items in Manchester, Stockport, Birkenhead, Liverpool, Chester, Sale and Knutsford. Turner's longest prison sentence was three years, which was handed down after her theft of a pair of boots from premises in Knutsford.

13 JUNE 1829 This week a man named Collier threw his wife – who was eight months pregnant – through a window. The woman was transferred to the infirmary, where it was expected that she would live.

14 JUNE 1906 Joseph and Sarah Ellen Galloway were tried at the Minshull Street Court for neglecting a 16-month-old child. It was claimed that their neglect resulted in the child's death. Joseph was employed as a porter and lived with his wife on Cowsill Street, Chorlton-on-Medlock. The child had been placed in their care because the mother – a lady named Florence Ridgway – had gone into the Withington Workhouse. The child was illegitimate, but the father was still involved in the child's life. When he heard that Florence was in the workhouse, he paid the Galloways three shillings per week to look after his child. Whilst in the couple's care, the child developed measles and pneumonia and died on 8 June. Medical inspectors who visited the child found that Joseph and Sarah were intoxicated. The inspectors instructed the couple to get medical help for the child, but they ignored their advice. At the inquest it was ruled that the child could have been saved if proper medical assistance had been given when the child first became ill. The couple were then sent for trial.

At the trial the pair made no excuses for their actions and were found guilty of child neglect. Sarah Galloway was sentenced to six months in prison with hard labour, and her husband was given three months.

15 JUNE 1835 On this day, two bricklayers named Owen Dempsey and Michael Goolding had an argument about who could carry the heaviest wheelbarrow filled with clay. The quarrel soon got heated and the pair began fighting. Dempsey appeared to be the aggressor and repeatedly hit Goolding. With the latter showing no resistance, Dempsey walked away. However, it was short-lived and it was not long before the pair were fighting again: Dempsey hit Goolding so hard that he fell to the floor. He then got up and went to hit him for the second time. By now, Goolding had managed to arm himself with a stone. As Dempsey got in range, Goolding threw the stone and hit him in the forehead. Goolding then attempted to flee but was caught by three men, who began attacking him. Holding his head in his hands, Dempsey then ran over and began kicking him while he was on the floor. Two men then intervened and carried Goolding into the local beerhouse. Dempsey was transferred to the infirmary, where he died as a result of a piece of bone from his skull piercing his brain.

An inquest was held on the following day, where it was ruled that Dempsey had died as a result of manslaughter. Such was the ill feeling towards Goolding from the community that he left his job and the area, and was not present at the inquest.

16 JUNE 1885 A 46-year-old man named John Welsh, who lived just off Deansgate, committed suicide after taking rat poison. It appears that Welsh had struggled to move on after the death of his wife eighteen months previous. On the day of the incident, he sent his son to the chemist to get some powders to kill vermin but, upon seeing the boy's age, the chemist refused to serve the boy and sent him back home. Welsh then went to the chemist and got them himself. Shortly after returning, he took the poison and became ill. His son went and fetched the doctor, who stated that he needed to go to the infirmary, but he died on the way.

17 JUNE 1879 An inquest into the death of Sarah Ann Thornley, who was brutally murdered by her husband, was held on this day. Sarah was married to a pawnbroker named Robert Thornley, who owned a shop on Gorton Lane. On the previous Sunday, the couple were residing in their flat above the shop, when without reason or warning, Mr Thornley picked up a razor and cut his wife's throat from ear to ear. He then left his dying wife and went to a neighbour's house to confess his crime. When the neighbour arrived, she saw Mrs Thornley lying on her side on the bedroom floor, with her back towards the fireplace and a large amount of blood on the floor and on the bed. Upon seeing the gruesome scene, the neighbour went and called for a constable. Robert Thornley was taken into custody and charged with the wilful murder of his wife.

18 JUNE 1880 Shortly after ten o'clock, a fire broke out at the India Mills on Bradford Road. A man named Charles Pooley, who owned a cotton spinning business, occupied the premises. Immediately after the fire was discovered, the fire brigade were called and arrived at fifteen minutes past ten.

The building was eight stories high. The fire broke out on the fifth floor, trapping those working on the floors above. The stranded workers had gathered at a window and seemed to be preparing to jump when the fire brigade arrived.

A group of onlookers attempted to assist the firemen by grabbing a fire escape and dragging it to the window where the workers were stranded. As they were pulling it across, the top of the escape got caught on a telephone wire that was attached to a chimney of a neighbouring shop. The fire escape then caused the chimney to collapse onto a 58-year-old woman named Eliza Woolford. She was immediately transferred to the infirmary, suffering from a serious head wound.

After an hour, the fire was brought under control and the workers were brought to safety. Eliza Woolford never regained consciousness and died later that afternoon of her injuries.

19 JUNE 1868 A 21-year-old man named Robert Wilkinson was brought up at the New Bailey charged with attempting to poison an elderly man named Charles Wolfenden in Gorton.

On 27 May, Wilkinson turned up at a farm at which Wolfenden was working and asked if there was any employment. The elderly man suggested he went and spoke to his brother, who owned the farm. Wilkinson then appeared to leave and Wolfenden carried on his work until his working day had finished. As he was leaving, he noticed that Wilkinson was waiting at the side of the road. As he passed him, the young man said that he would walk with him back to Gorton. On the way back, Wilkinson suggested the pair go for a drink because he was thirsty, so they decided to stop at the Bull's Head in Gorton. The young man went to the bar and ordered two glasses of beer, one of which he handed to Wolfenden. Immediately, Wolfenden was alerted to a black liquid that appeared to be floating on top of the drink. He put the drink to his mouth and was immediately overcome by the putrid taste of it. He then accused Wilkinson of trying to poison him. Wilkinson offered no explanation and fled the scene. The beer was given to the police and it was confirmed that the liquid was opium.

At the trial, Wolfenden said he later recognised the young man as the son of a woman who owned a life insurance policy in his name. Mrs Wilkinson held the £500 policy with the London Assurance Office. The jury listened to all of the evidence and found Wilkinson guilty of attempting to administer poison with the intent to murder; however, the jury recommended the young man to mercy on the grounds of his previous good character. The judge sentenced him to eighteen months in prison.

20 JUNE 1876 A woman named Margaret Cordingley was brought up at the County Police Court after she was caught selling beer during unlawful hours. Cordingley was the landlady of the Bridge Inn, Chortlon-cum-Hardy. She was twice caught selling beer to two undercover police officers during prohibited hours. Also in the beerhouse were two men who pretended to be travellers in order to get alcohol.

During the hearing, Mrs Cordingley stated to the bench that she had recently put into place measures to ensure only travellers were drinking during prohibited hours. After hearing the evidence, she was dismissed; however, the two fake travellers were fined five shillings plus costs for drinking after hours.

21 JUNE 1910 On this day, a serious accident occurred at the Bradford Colliery that resulted in the death of a man named Davies. The victim, along with a group of other men, had been working down the pit when a pony spooked and knocked down the props that were supporting the roof, which then began to cave in. All the men rushed to the exit but, when they reached the surface, they noticed that three men were missing. Fellow workers rushed to find the men and they were discovered buried in the debris. Davies died at the scene and the other two were transferred to the Ancoats Hospital, where it was expected that they would make a full recovery.

22 JUNE 1838 Early on Tuesday morning Mary Moore left her home in Fallowfield to make her usual three-mile trip to Smithfield Market. Mary, who went by the name 'Market Mary', had taken the same route for the past twenty years. She arrived at the market between six and seven o'clock in the morning and set up her stall just under the clock, selling farm produce for a Withington famer called Isaac Chorlton. Some time after one o'clock in the afternoon, Moore had sold all of her stock and began to head back to Withington. At approximately two o'clock she was spotted walking in the direction of her home and Mr Chorlton's farm. This was the last time she was seen alive.

After she failed to return to Mr Chorlton's farm, the alarm was raised that Mary was missing and a search party was gathered to find her. Tuesday came and went and she still had not been found. By Wednesday, the search party began to spread to Chorlton-cum-Hardy. A relative of Mary's began searching a pond in Hayson's Field, which is situated opposite Three Lane Ends. Near the pond was a ditch that was concealed by trees and bushes. When the men walked over to the ditch, they noticed the body of a woman lying face down in the water. After lifting her out, they noticed that the woman had suffered a series of severe blows to the right side of her head. A member of the search party identified the body as Mary Moore. The hunt then began to catch her killer.

After an extensive investigation, four men were arrested on suspicion of robbery and murder, although at a later trial three men were released without charge. William Hodge, a gardener who had worked for the late Mrs Chorlton, was found guilty of Mary's murder. It was believed that he had been unemployed since the death of Mrs Chorlton. Hodge and Moore were work colleagues at the farm and he was familiar with her schedule on market days. On the day in question, he was identified by three witnesses, who stated that they saw him hiding something in the bushes where Mary was found. Hodge was subsequently sent to the South Lancashire Summer Assizes, where he was remarkably found not guilty of her murder. The murderer was never caught.

23 JUNE 1828 On this day, a young boy was playing in the streets of Ancoats when a mysterious lady approached him and asked him to deliver a fruit cake to a man called Mr Drummond. Drummond was a flour and provision dealer, who lived a short walk away on Richmond Street. The boy agreed and the lady paid him two sixpences for his trouble. Arriving at the house, he handed Mrs Drummond the cake and relayed the message that the cake was a gift from Mrs McCann. Having never heard of a 'Mrs McCann', Mrs Drummond attempted to give the cake back but the boy insisted that it was meant for her family.

Later on that day, the boy went and told his mother the story, explaining that he had got two sixpences for his trouble. Thinking that he might have stolen the money, his mother went to speak to Mrs Drummond to confirm what her son had told her. Mrs Drummond, convinced that the cake was not for her, handed it to the boy's mother. On the way home, she began handing out pieces of the cake to her neighbours and their children, as well as her own. As soon as they swallowed the cake, people began to complain of a burning sensation in the mouth and throat, which was followed by vomiting. Two of the children and an old woman were transferred to the infirmary. One of the children, 4-year-old Susannah Rigby, died as a result of eating the cake. Tests later confirmed that the cake was laced with arsenic and the consumption of even a small slice would have been enough to kill. It was believed that the others only survived because they were sick and the poison was therefore expelled.

With no one arrested, the police offered a reward to catch the mysterious 'Mrs McCann'. She was described as being of medium height, with big front teeth. She was wearing a brown gown with a black bonnet and a light-coloured shawl. The suspected poisoner also had a baby in her arms.

24 JUNE 1911 Robert and Annie Kelly, who lived on Jenkinson Street, Chorlton-on-Medlock, were sent to prison for neglecting their three children. A witness at the trial stated that when he arrived at the Kelly family home, the smell was unbearable. He further commented that two of the children were sat on a dirty bed, which was infested with vermin. The children were wearing barely any clothes and their bodies were covered in ulcers. The eldest child was so malnourished that he could not walk. The woman was sentenced to six months in prison and the father to four months.

25 JUNE 1893 On this night, two boys named Albert and Frederick Bannister were caught midway through robbing a shop in Gorton. Albert (15) and Frederick (10) were the sons of a travelling draper named Walter. The family resided at a house on Haigh Street in Gorton.

The two boys had decided to rob the grocery store of Mr Stables, which was situated on Gorton Road. Whilst in the process of committing their crime, the boys made a loud noise that attracted the attention of the local residents, who then apprehended the would-be thieves. A quick examination of the shop found that they had gained entry by opening a window at the rear of the property. After making their way inside, the pair had quickly put together some goods that they were ready to steal.

The two boys were brought up at the City Police Court on 27 June. The bench found them both guilty. Albert – who had a previous conviction – was sentenced to twenty-one days in prison, followed by five years in a reformatory. (Reformatories were similar to young offenders' institutes. They offered offenders career training, physical exercise, schooling and lessons in how to be a 'good' citizen, which included studies on religion and morals.) Frederick was ordered to be birched. Birching was similar to the cane: a birch rod was used to hit the offender on a said part of the body – normally the bare buttock. He was also instructed to attend the Mill Street Industrial Day School.

26 JUNE 1902 The good people of Manchester were celebrating the accession of King Edward VII to the British throne. After the death of Queen Victoria in 1901, palace officials had scheduled the coronation of Edward for 26 June. All the preparations were in place when the future king was taken ill with an abdominal abscess. Acknowledging that the new king would not be well enough for the coronation, the palace decided to postpone the ceremony until 9 August 1902. However, celebrations were held throughout Britain to mark the original date for the coronation of the king.

In Manchester, James and Elizabeth Wilson had also been celebrating on that day. The couple lived in the single room of a property on Grove Street, off Garside Street, which was situated in the district of Deansgate. This area was one of the poorest in the city.

On that evening, a large number of residents who lived on Grove Street were having a street party. Mr Wilson – otherwise known as 'Jewellery Jack' because of his occupation as a jewellery hawker – had been enjoying the festivities and appeared intoxicated. At some point in the evening, the couple returned to their home and Mr Wilson asked his wife to go and fetch him more beer. When she returned, the couple began arguing. The events after this are unclear; however, the following morning, Mrs Wilson's bruised and battered body was discovered in the house. Mr Wilson was not present at the time of the discovery, as he had gone to the pub to get more alcohol, leaving the dead woman in the house. He was arrested and sent to the police station, where he was charged with the wilful murder of his wife.

27 JUNE 1884 On this day, a man named James Lee was brought up at the City Police Court charged with stealing a silver watch from an insurance agent. On the evening of 5 June, the agent was leaving Belle Vue Gardens when he was violently pushed to the floor. When he had recovered, he discovered that his watch had been stolen. After realising that he had been seen, Lee attempted to disappear into the crowds and make his escape. However, later that day he was apprehended and taken into custody. Whilst the police officer was holding him, Lee was seen to hand the watch to another man named Gillard. Both men were taken to the police station to await their trial. On 6 June they were taken before the bench and remanded to appear on 13 June. Both men listened to the court and then calmly began to walk down to the cells, however as they reached the steps, the pair fled through an open door and disappeared into the street. Lee was later recaptured and sent for trial at the sessions. Gillard was never caught.

28 JUNE 1856 At nine o'clock, William Bates and Samuel Taylor were walking down George Street in Hulme when they spotted two brothers named James and Andrew Bracken chasing a man into the Brown Cow beer shop. The two men attempted to intervene, but were then set upon by the two brothers. Taylor managed to escape, but Bates was trapped. Andrew Bracken punched Bates, knocking him to the floor, and then both brothers began kicking him about the head. The attack only stopped when the two brothers saw some police officers running towards them. The victim died of his injuries. The post-mortem revealed that death occurred as a result of a fracture of the skull, which led to a fatal bleed on the brain.

The two brothers were arrested and sent to trial at the Liverpool Assizes on 18 August for the wilful murder of William Bates. The jury heard evidence from the defence and prosecution and found James Bracken guilty of manslaughter, while deciding that Andrew Bracken was guilty of murder. Upon hearing the news, James collapsed in the dock. When he came around, he screamed for God to have mercy on his brother. The mother and sisters of the accused man shrieked in horror as the verdict was read out, and all had to be taken outside. Struggling to contain his emotions, the judge placed the black cap on his head. Quietly sobbing, he stated that he would ask for mercy for the man on the grounds that he was intoxicated at the time, but held little hope that the man's life would be spared. He then sentenced Andrew Bracken to death, specifying that his body should be buried within the gaol.

After several appeals by members of the public and a recommendation from the judge, Bracken's sentence was reduced to life imprisonment.

29 JUNE 1910 A labourer named Frederick Taylor, alias Patrick Quinn, was serving a fourteen-day prison sentence for stealing. By the end of 1915, he had seven convictions for stealing and one conviction for loitering with intent. His crime spree only ended after he signed up to join the war effort.

30 JUNE 1924 An inquest was held on the body of 35-year-old Richard Rattigan Hugo, who was found dead in the well of a hoist. Hugo worked as a racker at Boddington's Brewery, Strangeways and lived on Holgate Street in Hulme.

The circumstances that led him to be in the well are unclear. One colleague suggested that he could have started the hoist before he got into it and when he stepped inside, his foot fell through and he ended up trapped.

After hearing all the evidence, the coroner ruled that the death was accidental.

JULY

1 JULY 1852 A 36-year-old architect named William Fern died after briefly being admitted to the Manchester Workhouse.

Earlier that evening Fern had been drinking. Fuelled by alcohol, he took the decision to end his life by slitting his throat. A man named George Osborne – who lived with the architect – witnessed him stagger through the door of his room and then fall to the floor. He was bleeding heavily from the wound to his neck. Osborne immediately summoned the local doctor and Fern was transferred to the infirmary.

Once at the hospital, Fern was examined and deemed to be mentally unstable. He was placed in a straitjacket and his legs were bound together. The House of Apothecary recommended that he be transferred to the lunatic asylum at a cost to the surgeon that brought him in, but the doctor refused to pay and so the patient was taken to the workhouse.

He arrived at the workhouse by cab, but the dying man was not allowed to enter the institution until a porter had concluded a meeting with the Prestwich Union and the infirmary. In the event, Fern was restrained on his stretcher for over two hours, being eventually admitted at half-past eleven in the evening.

A surgeon examined the architect, but it was too late, and he died at four o'clock the following morning. The cause of death was diagnosed as a bleed on the brain, which was probably caused by the fall.

At the inquest, the coroner requested an inquiry into the practices of the establishments and its officers, to determine if anyone could be held accountable for the poor treatment of William Fern.

2 JULY 1352 In this year, a deadly plague attacked the residents of the city. Although no specifics of the type of plague have survived, it was believed that it was a strain of the Black Death that had killed millions of people throughout Europe. A person suffering from the disease was said to experience an acute fever, vomiting and a swelling of the lymph nodes in the armpit, groin and neck. Once the lymph nodes were swollen, they would then burst, and pus and blood would ooze out of them. The disease also caused the skin to die and turn black. A painful death would usually occur within seven days of contracting the disease.

3 JULY 1884 Two men were killed at the Old School Mill, Victoria Station. The deceased were named as 25-year-old Peter Morgan and 43-year-old Joseph Richie. The pair had been removing rubbish from one of the arches in the mill when another worker warned them that cracks had appeared in the wall of the arch. The two men carried on working when, without warning, the arch collapsed, crushing the men under a pile of bricks. By the time Morgan and Richie were pulled from the debris, they were in a very bad way. The pair were immediately transferred to the Royal Infirmary, where they later died of their injuries.

4 JULY 1862 Two bailiffs named William Stubbs and John Fox arrived at the home of picker-maker William Blackledge to remove his property.

Blackledge and his family lived on Daniel Street, which was in the Bradford district of Manchester. For some weeks previous, he had struggled to find work, which had caused him to fall behind on the rent. His landlord warned him that bailiffs would be sent to the house to seize goods up to the value of the missed rent.

After arriving at the house, the two men set to work to remove the furniture. Filled with rage, Blackledge picked up a knife and lunged at the two men, wounding them both. Stubbs and Fox were bleeding heavily and were transferred to the infirmary, while Blackledge was arrested and later sent for trial at the assizes. He was sentenced to three years' penal servitude.

5 JULY 1642 A fight broke out between the inhabitants of Manchester and the King's Troops. The Royalists lost over twenty men, and the residents eleven. Manchester remained loyal to the Roundheads.

1858 An inquest was held into the death of 25-year-old Catherine McCarty, who died in the New Bridge Street Workhouse. Catherine had been living with her four children and husband in the cellar of Court 1, Addington Street. Catherine was employed as a basket maker and paid her landlord two shillings a week in rent. After her husband was sent to prison, her life took a drastic turn for the worse. She could no longer afford to pay her rent or put food on the table for her children. Fearing for Catherine's safety, a neighbour called the Inspector of Lodging Houses to check on the conditions in which the woman and her children were living. Upon entering the cellar, the inspector was greeted with such a putrid stench that he felt physically sick. The inspector had never before witnessed such a foul sight. Catherine was lying on the bed, wearing only a petticoat. The only thing covering the bed was an old horse cloth. There was no furniture in the room and maggots and other vermin swarmed the bed.

Catherine and the children were taken from the room and placed in the workhouse. Sometime the same evening Catherine died. The superintendent of the medical ward stated that he had never witnessed anyone in such a disgusting condition.

The coroner ruled that Catherine McCarty died of phthisis (pulmonary tuberculosis), which she had acquired in both lungs.

6 JULY 1825 On this day, Charles Green was sat in his cell in Lancaster Castle awaiting trial for the murder of his mother – a charge that was later reduced to manslaughter. The events that led to his charge began on the evening of 25 June. The Green family and a visitor named Martha Reed were sat at home in the district of Piccadilly, when they heard a knock at the door. Margaret Green opened the door and was greeted by her son, Charles. The young man barged his way into the house, ran straight up to his father and threatened him. Fearing for his safety, his father fled the house, leaving Margaret and Martha alone with the crazed man. Margaret attempted to calm her son by instructing him to sit down, but he refused. Instead he turned to his mother and punched her in the face, knocking her to the floor. While she lay helpless on the ground, he repeatedly kicked her. Martha tried to leave, but Charles grabbed hold of her and knocked her down, giving her a black eye.

A few days later, Mrs Green died from her injuries. She had suffered several broken ribs and a ruptured spleen, which had caused her death.

7 JULY 1775 Manchester's ducking stool was used for punishing prostitutes. The contraption was suspended over the infirmary pond at Piccadilly, which used to be known as Daub Holes. It had formally been situated at Pool Fold (where Cross Street is today). The ducking stool was an open-bottomed wooden chair, which was attached

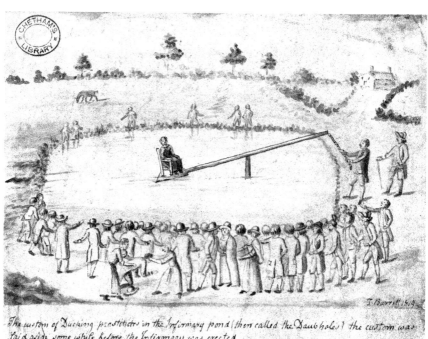

The custom of Ducking prostitutes in the Infirmary pond (then called the Daub holes) the custom was laid aside some while before the Infirmary was erected

to a long pole on a pivot. The prostitute would have been strapped to the chair and then dunked into the cold water as a form of punishment.

8 JULY 1836 This week, several newspapers reported on the tragic death of 23-year-old Isabella Paton, who owned Paton and McMillan Milliners & Co., Faulkner Street.

On Friday evening, the young woman bent down to pick up some cotton that had fallen on the floor. In her hand was a piece of work that she was finishing. As Isabella reached for the cotton, her work caught fire. Thinking quickly, she threw it on the floor and began to stamp out the flames. The work was nearly extinguished when the flames caught her dress, setting her on fire. Witnessing the horrific event was Isabella's younger sister who, in an attempt to extinguish the fire, tried to push her to the floor. Isabella resisted, however, and ran downstairs. A passer-by heard the screams and managed to force his way into the house. He tried in vain to put out the flames with his coat, but it was too late. Isabella Paton was so severely burned that she died of her injuries two days later.

9 JULY 1915 An inquest was held at the Coroner's Court in Manchester into the death of 47-year-old Hannah Kennedy.

On 2 July, Mrs Kennedy and her husband Daniel were at their home on Whyatt Street, Bradford, when they got into an argument. According to a witness, the couple were arguing over Daniel's refusal to find employment.

Intoxicated and filled with rage, Daniel picked up an oil lamp and threw it at his wife. After hitting her body, the lamp smashed and the flames set her on fire. The drunken man attempted to get some water but slipped and hit his head. The flames were only extinguished when some neighbours entered the house and saw Hannah burning. She was transferred to Ancoats Hospital but later died. The coroner ruled that a charge of manslaughter should be brought against Daniel, and he was held in custody until his trial.

On 15 July, he appeared at the Crown Court and was found guilty of manslaughter. He was sentenced to eighteen months in prison with hard labour.

10 JULY 1903 On this morning, 9-year-old Sarah Fletcher and her 4-year-old sister, Christina Fletcher, were in bed at their family home on Henry Street when their house collapsed, trapping them in the debris. Their house was one of three that were destroyed after a chimneystack fell in between numbers 109 and 111.

The children's mother and father managed to scramble their way to safety but the girls were trapped. Later that day, the bodies of Sarah and Christina were pulled out of the debris.

Several inquests were held throughout July and the coroner eventually ruled that the accident was caused by criminal neglect, stating that the landlord had not maintained the house properly. The agent for the property, Walter Warnes, was summoned to appear at the City Police Court, charged with manslaughter.

11 JULY 1847 A chimney sweep by the name of Thomas Price died in the most shocking of circumstances. He was the son of Thomas and Elizabeth Price, who lived on Shipley Street. At the time of his death, he was residing at the home of his employer, a master sweeper called John Gordon.

On this particular day, Price was working with his master, cleaning out some flues that were attached to a furnace, when he realised that the flue was too hot to continue sweeping. His employer forced him to carry on even though the young sweep was now struggling to breathe because of the dense soot. The soot was so hot that it was on fire in parts of the flue. After ten minutes, another sweep entered the flue and found the boy face down in the soot. He carried him out and a wet cloth was placed on his head. The young boy was then transferred – in a bag – to the basement of Gordon's house. Once there, he began to suffer a fit, hitting his head very hard. Gordon accused the young sweep of faking his illness to avoid working and summoned his wife to fetch a rod. He then pulled up the young boy's shirt and beat him on the back, only stopping when his wife intervened. Gordon then left and went back to the chimney. The young boy later died of his injuries.

The inquest was held two days after his death, at the Red Lion pub in London Road. The post-mortem was inconclusive in revealing the cause of death: the surgeon could not determine if suffocation or a convulsion killed Price. The deceased's body also revealed that he had suffered regular beatings from his master.

After hearing the evidence, the jury found Gordon guilty of manslaughter and he was sent for trial. His trial was heard at the South Lancashire Assizes in August where, after a short deliberation, the jury found him guilty. He was sentenced to ten years' transportation. In summing up, the judge expressed the hope that the sentence would act as a deterrent to anyone else who ill-treated his or her employees.

12 JULY 1859 Two girls named Mary O'Hare and Agnes Mooney were brought up at the City Police Court charged with stealing a large quantity of ostrich feathers.

Some three months previous, O'Hare had left her native Liverpool and come to Manchester to seek employment. She managed to find work with Elizabeth Tyrer, a feather manufacturer with premises on Edge Street. Initially the girl worked extremely hard and Tyrer was very impressed. Such was their relationship that when another position became available, O'Hare recommended her friend Agnes Mooney, and the girl was taken on. The girls worked very hard until Whit-week, when it was alleged that they met some undesirable acquaintances and became unmanageable.

On the previous Saturday, Tyrer asked the girls to fetch some feathers and meet her at the fete at Ordsal Gardens. She waited by the gate but the girls never arrived; they had stolen just short of a hundred feathers and were on their way back to Liverpool. The police were immediately called and went to O'Hare's mother's house, where they found the girls and the feathers. Both girls pleaded guilty and were sentenced to three months in prison.

13 JULY 1880 Manchester was in the midst of being battered by a ferocious thunderstorm. Annie Harriet Jones, the 17-year-old daughter of a traveller, had braved the weather that day and was working in her uncle's shop. Her uncle was a tobacconist and owned a shop at 12 Albert Place, Albert Bridge.

As the day progressed, the weather worsened and by the afternoon, thunder could be heard throughout the city. Without warning, a bolt of lightning hit the shops on Albert Place with such force that it caused the buildings to collapse into the river, trapping several people under the debris. A rescue operation got underway and the first two bodies to be pulled from the rubble were those of hairdresser Thomas Fildes and grocer William Way. Annie was still missing, however. Her body was not discovered until the following day. She had been trapped face down in the water by the falling debris.

14 JULY 1874 On this day, one of Manchester's 'most dangerous' thieves was on the run after stealing £50 in money and jewellery from Huddersfield. He was described as being 43 years old and five feet eight inches tall with a stout build, blotched face and with reddish whiskers. He often went by the name Charlie Mullen, although he had several aliases.

Charlie Mullen, one of Manchester's most feared criminals

15 JULY 1851 A painter was working at the home of William Durham when he discovered the gruesome remains of a child hidden in a basket. The workman was in the cellar when a servant named Alice Milligan came to him to ask if he wanted the basket removing from the room. The man replied no and the woman left. Concerned by her manner, he decided to take a look inside the basket and, upon opening it, he discovered a large quantity of rubbish. As he dug beneath, he found the body of a newborn child. Horrified by the discovery, he fled the cellar and went to the Town Hall, where he met the chief superintendent of the police. After relaying the story to him, the superintendent sent an officer to the house. By the time the policeman arrived, however, the body was missing and the two servants – Alice Milligan and Catherine Nixon – denied all knowledge of the missing infant. Not believing their story, the officer arrested Milligan and transported her to the lock-up. Later that evening, she admitted that the child was hers and upon its discovery by the painter, she flushed it down the water closet. She was then held in custody on a charge of the concealment and murder of her child.

16 JULY 1890 A joiner named Edward Young was sentenced to death for the murder of his 34-year-old wife, Esther. Young, his wife and four children lived on Worrall Street, which is situated just off Rochdale Road.

The couple had a volatile relationship. The previous year, Young had spent three months in prison for assaulting her. Upon his release, he seemed to have changed his ways, but at the start of the year he had begun to threaten his wife again.

On the evening of 20 June, the couple were heard arguing by their children. It appears that the argument was caused by Young's refusal to stop smoking in bed. Shortly after midnight, one of the children heard screams coming from their parents' bedroom. The girl rushed to see what was wrong and discovered her mother covered in blood, holding a child in her arms. She was quite dead. Esther Young had been killed by a cut to the throat and chest with a shoemaker's knife.

Young was later arrested and committed for trial at the Manchester Assizes. His defence attempted to claim that he was insane at the time of the crime, but the jury disagreed and the judge sentenced him to death for the murder of his wife.

17 JULY 1835 This day saw a servant named Ann Brown brought up at the New Bailey by her master – a man named Mr Barker of Strangeways.

On the night of the incident, Barker returned home and found his door bolted shut. He banged on the door but no one answered so he enlisted the help of a young boy, who climbed over the wall and gained entry to the property. Once inside, Barker found Brown drunk and with her dress on fire. It appeared that she was so intoxicated that she did not realise that she was on fire. Barker claimed that this was not Brown's first offence: some weeks previous, she had been drunk and had set fire to her bed.

After hearing the evidence, she was discharged of any criminal activity; however, she was sacked by Mr Barker.

18 JULY 1922 An inquest was held into the death of 9-month-old Mary Ellen Fancourt, the daughter of Wilfred Fancourt. Wilfred and his family lived on Church Lane, Harpurhey. On 6 July, Mrs Fancourt was rushing across Exchange Street when she failed to see an oncoming car. In her arms was her daughter, who fell onto the road and suffered a fractured skull. She died a short time later.

Although the driver appeared to be travelling faster than the advisable speed limit, it was argued that if the woman was not carrying an umbrella, she might have seen the car. After listening to the evidence, the jury ruled that the death was accidental.

19 JULY 1879 Several newspapers across the country reported on the trial of a Fenian named John O'Reilly, who was accused of shooting a man named Frederick Dove in Lever Street on 17 May. Dove and the accused man were both members of a secret organisation called the Home Rule Association. At the trial it was alleged that the group was really a Fenian society: an accusation that O'Reilly refused to deny.

On the night of the incident, Dove was returning home after a day selling his glassware when he was set upon by four men. The assailants appeared from a dark passage and had their faces covered. One of the men produced a gun and shot Dove four times before the group fled. A passer-by who witnessed the shooting chased the attackers until one of the men threatened to shoot him if he continued to pursue them. Dove was transferred to the infirmary, where he later recovered.

At the trial, O'Reilly had several witnesses who stated that he was nowhere near the crime scene at the time of the attack. After hearing all the evidence the jury found the man not guilty and he was discharged.

20 JULY 1882 A shocking occurrence happened shortly before dinnertime at a house on St Leonard's Street, Chorlton-upon-Medlock. Living in the house was a woman called Ellen Howard, who often went by the name Ada Howard. It appeared that Ellen had a questionable reputation when it came to men. In 1882, she had used her charm to seduce a young man named Montague Newby.

Montague was 21 years old and was born into a very well-respected family. His father Alfred was a clergyman who lived in Yorkshire with Montague's mother and siblings. The family lived comfortably, employing two servants.

Montague arrived in Manchester in 1880, having secured employment with one of Manchester's most prestigious law firms. In 1881, he met and fell in love with Ellen Howard. He quickly became infatuated with her, writing her love letters in the hope that they would marry.

On the night in question, Montague was in Ellen's house and the pair began arguing about her relationship with another man whom she was planning to marry. It is believed that she then asked Montague to leave and declared that she did not love him. Devastated, he went upstairs and returned carrying a gun. Upon seeing the weapon, Ellen pleaded with him not to pull the trigger, but he did not listen and instantly fired a shot into her head. The bullet entered her head behind the left ear and exited at the back of her skull, exposing her brain and killing her instantly. Montague then pointed the revolver to the right side of his head and fired. The autopsy on the two bodies was scheduled for the next day.

21 **JULY** 1900 James Ferriman and John Hawton were playing snooker in the billiard room of Liston's Bar when they heard a band playing outside. The two men decided to go to the window and have a listen. A fellow billiard player warned them to stay away from the window because the ledge was not safe. However, the pair did not listen and,

resting on the ledge, the pair then began throwing coppers into the street. They had only been there a short while when it suddenly gave way and the pair were sent crashing onto the pavement below. Both Ferriman and Hawton died of their injuries. At the inquest, the coroner returned a verdict of accidental death.

22 JULY 1851 On this day, a farm labourer named James Wick was brought before the Police Court charged with the murder of Margaret Weldon. Margaret lived with her friend Ellen Farrand in the cellar of a property on Back Irwell Street.

On the previous Sunday evening, Margaret left her house and returned later that evening with James Wick. Under the influence of drink, Wick gave both of the women a shilling, then removed his trousers and went to bed. Some time later he awoke and found himself alone in the house. Searching through his pockets, he could not find four half-crowns. With the women and the money missing, he assumed that he had been robbed.

When the ladies returned to the house, Wick grabbed them both and began a savage attack, throwing them to the ground and kicking and punching them. The assault only stopped after a police constable – who heard the women shout for help – intervened. The constable managed to stop the prisoner escaping while he summoned for back-up.

When assistance arrived, the constable tried to help the women. Weldon was lying face down on the floor. Her injuries were so severe that she died before medical assistance could be given. Farrand was still alive, but bleeding heavily from wounds to her face. She was transferred to the infirmary, where it was hoped that she would recover.

At the port-mortem, the surgeon revealed that Weldon died of internal injuries. The blows had been delivered with such force that they lacerated her liver, caused fractures on both side of her ribs and collapsed one of her lungs. The jury at the inquest found Wick guilty of the wilful murder of Margaret Weldon and he was committed for trial.

23 JULY 1907 On this day, a father named William Grimshaw attempted to murder his two sons, William and Harry Alexander Grimshaw (aged 6 and 4, respectively), by throwing them through the attic window of their three-storey home. Grimshaw, who lived with his family on Exeter Street, Ardwick, is said to have been intoxicated at the time. Witnesses stated that on the evening in question, Grimshaw returned home and went upstairs to see his children. His wife and brother-in-law then heard screams coming from the yard. When they ran outside, they found the bodies of the two boys lying on the ground, severely injured. The youngest child was in the worst condition; the fall had fractured his head and the doctors felt that he would not survive.

A washing line had broken the fall of his brother and it was hoped that he would recover. Miraculously however, both boys survived.

Grimshaw was tried at the assizes in October. He was found guilty of attempted murder and sentenced to five years' penal servitude.

24 JULY 1879 A brutal murder occurred at the County Lunatic Asylum in Prestwich. The victim was a 60-year-old inmate by the name of John Cheetham. He had been a resident of the asylum for twenty-eight years.

The tragic events unfolded in the morning, when John and a few other inmates were working in the field. Without warning or reason, another inmate called John McGee picked up an iron bar and stuck him across the head. The blow was delivered with such force that it fractured his skull, killing him instantly.

McGee, 49, had been a patient in the asylum for nine years. Prior to this incident, he had been regarded as a quiet man who posed no threat to patients or staff.

The jury at the inquest ruled that McGee was insane when he committed the crime. He was then removed from his padded cell and transferred to Broadmoor.

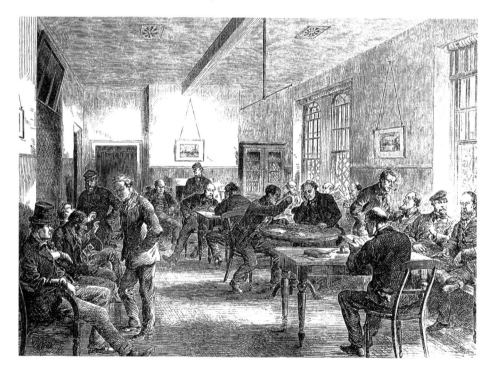

25 JULY 1848 On this day, Diana Thomas left her father's house on Oldham Road and began her usual walk to Hanover Mills, where she was in employment. Upon

reaching Lever Street, she bumped into a man named William Adams. Some weeks previous, Adams and Mrs Thomas had been in a relationship. Adams begged Diana to reunite with him, but she refused. He then attempted to grab her, but she screamed and managed to escape. Fearing for her safety, Diana started running up Friday Street, with Adams in pursuit. He eventually caught her and grabbed her by her clothes. He then produced a gun and fired a bullet into her head. The first shot missed, so he tried again. The second bullet found its target and Diana fell to the floor and died a short time later.

Adams was brought before the Borough Court and it was revealed that the couple had been married, but had separated and had new partners. Diana's husband was in prison, but he was due for release soon. Adams was also married and had two children.

After all the evidence was heard, Adams was transferred to Liverpool Assizes, where he stood trial for the wilful murder of Diana Thomas. After hearing the evidence, the jury found him guilty and he was sentenced to death. On 16 September, he was executed by Mr Calcraft at Kirkdale Gaol. His body was then interred in the grounds of the gaol.

26 JULY 1859 Peter Ford and brothers John Thomas and William Irving drowned in a pit at Moss Side. The two brothers were the sons of a city missionary called John Irving, who resided on Boundary Street, Hulme.

William, just 10 years old, was swimming in the pit – which was part of Peter Botham's farm – when he got into difficulty. The farm was situated at the top of Upper Moss Lane, which was on the border of Moss Side and Hulme.

Realising that his brother was in trouble, John jumped in to rescue him. As John made his way closer to his brother, he too began to sink into the mud and was struggling to keep his head above the water. They both screamed for help. A labourer who was working on the next farm heard their cries and jumped into the water to try and save them. He managed to grab both of the boys, but their combined weight was too much for him to hold and all three of them began to sink. Two other labourers who were working with Ford attempted to retrieve all three from the water, but they were unable to reach them. By the time the bodies were eventually pulled from the pit, two were already dead. One of the victims was showing slight signs of life, but he also died a short time later.

27 JULY 1908 On this day, a 'mothers' meeting' convoy of three coaches from Hulme left the Bridgewater Mission Hall to attend a picnic in Mottram. As they were travelling down a steep hill near Broadbottom Station, the driver attempted to pull

the brake but one of the horses spooked, which in turn set off the other two horses. All three horses were now galloping down the hill. As they reached the foot of the hill there was a sharp curve, which caused one of the horses to slip and brought them all to the ground, overturning the vehicle in the process. All the passengers were thrown on the road.

The police and local medical professionals were quickly on the scene and transported the seriously injured to the Royal Infirmary. In total, twenty-one people needed medical assistance. The driver, a man named James Farthing of Carey Street, Hulme, suffered life-changing injuries. He had a compound fracture of his arm, which resulted in it being amputated. A passenger named Sarah Ann Chapman of Church Street, Hulme, also suffered serious injuries after she fractured her skull.

28 JULY 1846 An inquest was held before the borough coroner on the body of a 31-year-old tassel maker named Elizabeth Bickerton. Elizabeth had come to Manchester from Macclesfield to seek regular employment. She resided with a man named James Hunt, who was also a native of Macclesfield. The couple were renting two rooms in the attic of No. 34 Cable Street, which was situated just off Rochdale Road.

Hunt and Bickerton were known to like a drink. Neighbours reported that the pair regularly argued and even engaged in physical fights.

On the previous Saturday evening, Elizabeth returned home from a walk and was confronted by an angry Hunt. He accused her of being with another man, which led to an argument. Hunt was filled with rage and, without warning, he clenched his fist and hit his lover in the side of the head. Bickerton fell to the floor and died instantly. Hunt quickly fled the scene, but was later found at the house of a Jane Poole. At the inquest, the jury found him guilty of manslaughter and he was sent for trial.

29 JULY 1848 This week an 11-year-old boy named George Roe was sentenced at the Borough Court to three months' hard labour for stealing. Roe had stolen some books from the pocket of a teenager named Joseph Harley, who was sleeping in the street. Roe, who was known to the police, was caught in the act by a passing officer and transferred to the local police station.

30 JULY 1746 John Berwick, a lieutenant in the Manchester Regiment, and Andrew Blood, an officer in the Manchester Squadron, were executed at Kennington Common. The men were part of a group of soldiers that was executed after being found guilty of treason during the Jacobite Rebellion in 1745. The men had been captured during a battle in Carlisle. In total, nine of the Manchester Regiment were executed. The men

were awoken at six o'clock in the morning and led to the gallows. A rope was then placed around each man's neck and they were hung for three minutes. Their bodies were then beheaded and disembowelled, and their viscera was thrown on a fire. Their heads were transported to Manchester and placed outside the Exchange.

1878 Antonio Leary, one of the country's most notorious criminals, was back behind bars on this day, after being caught loitering at Victoria Street Station. He was charged, along with another man, with intending to commit a felony.

Leary's forty-five-year crime spree stretched across the country. Under a number of aliases, it was revealed that he had spent time in prisons in Bath, Birmingham, Bristol, Manchester, London and Kirkdale. He also spent fourteen years on board a hulk ship

in Chatham, where he stabbed a warder who later died. In 1858 and 1870 he was committed to Broadmoor Criminal Lunatic Asylum. Leary had spent the whole of his adult life committing crime.

For his most recent arrest, he was sentenced to six months' hard labour. His accomplice was sentenced to two months' hard labour.

31 JULY 1880 Several newspapers reported on the inquest into the death of 17-year-old Alice Ann Hall, who was discovered in the Rochdale Canal on 17 July.

A witness said that he had seen the woman on the night of her disappearance in the company of a man named Thomas Mayne. By all accounts, Mayne and Hall had been dating for some time, but the relationship appeared to be strained, with reports that Mayne had hit Hall on several occasions.

On the night of the incident, the couple were seen at the Friendship Inn enjoying a drink. Mayne was so intoxicated that the landlord banned him from buying liquor. The couple then left and were seen walking alongside the Rochdale Canal. A nightwatchman recalled seeing Thomas with his arm around Alice; she was crying. He then stated that he saw the man push her in the water. The witness shouted to Mayne to help her out, but he left in the direction of Hulme Hall Lane Bridge.

Mayne was later apprehended by the police on suspicion of murder. On 5 November, he faced a trial at the Liverpool Assizes. In his defence, he denied that he pushed her in, stating that she jumped in herself. The jury listened to the evidence and found him not guilty. He was then acquitted and free to go home.

AUGUST

1   AUGUST   1890   An inquest was held into the death of a 2-year-old girl named Martha Ann Partington. Martha was at the family home on Abel Street, Collyhurst, when she pulled a cup of boiling tea on top of herself. The hot liquid severely scalded her chest. She was given medical assistance, but her condition deteriorated and she died two weeks later. After hearing the evidence, the jury found that the child's death was accidental and decided that no further action would be taken.

2   AUGUST   1831   A woman named Mary Sherworth committed suicide by throwing herself through a third-storey window. At the inquest, it was revealed that the woman had been suffering from 'low spirits' due to her husband having recently deserted her and her daughter emigrating to America. The jury recorded a verdict of lunacy.

3   AUGUST   1604–06   Manchester was gripped by an epidemic that seemed to be similar to the plague. Contemporary reports suggested that in the two years that the plague was at its peak, it killed 2,000 people (although this could be a slight exaggeration). A plot of land in Collyhurst was donated by Rowland Mosley to bury the dead.

4   AUGUST   1855   Maria Calloway was returning from Belle Vue Gardens when she bumped into her estranged husband on the corner of Devonshire Street. Mr Calloway had just been released from Lancaster Castle, after spending three years inside for debt owed to his father-in-law.

The ballroom at Belle Vue Gardens.

Upon seeing each other, the couple got into an argument. In the midst of the row, Mr Calloway knocked Maria to the floor and produced a knife. He then repeatedly stabbed his wife in the throat, back of the neck and arm. Mrs Calloway, who was now bleeding heavily, began to shout for help. Two men heard her screams and rushed over to help. She was taken to the druggist's shop and then transferred to the infirmary.

Mr Calloway was tried at the assizes on 24 August. He was found guilty of wounding his wife with the intent to disable. He was sentenced to fifteen years in prison.

5 AUGUST 1896 On this day, newspapers across the country reported on the execution of 26-year-old James Hurst that had taken place in Manchester the previous day.

On 2 April, Hurst had been tried and convicted of murdering the illegitimate 3-month-old daughter of his partner. The child's mother was a woman named Martha Ann Goddard.

On the day of the incident, she returned to their home in Chorlton-upon-Medlock and was met by Hurst, who stated that he had murdered the infant by strangling her around the neck. The pair then went to the Ashton Canal, tied a piece of string with a rock attached around the child's neck and threw her into the water. The pair then fled.

The child was discovered on 4 April. The couple were found two months later living in Leicester. After their arrest, they were transported back to Manchester, where Hurst confessed to the crime. Goddard was arrested, but the charges were dropped after she agreed to testify against Hurst.

6 AUGUST 1851 A 9-year-old boy named John Walton was killed after being run over by a cab. John and his friends were hanging onto the back of a lurry (a four-wheeled wagon that was pulled by horses) travelling along Deansgate, heading towards Hulme. The boys jumped off the vehicle opposite Liverpool Road to head home. Whilst they were crossing Deansgate, John was knocked over by a cab. The wheels went over his body, crushing it in the process. Rather than stopping at the scene, the driver of the cab whipped his horse and sped off. The young boy was taken home, where he died the following day of his injuries.

7 AUGUST 1876 A dreadful murder occurred on this night at a house on Hanover Street. The victim was 45-year-old widow Mary Ann Hartshorn. The murderer was named as 60-year-old George Jackson, who had arrived in Manchester on the morning of the crime.

The victim had met the man sometime in the afternoon and the pair decided to spend the day drinking together. Some time in the evening, the couple went to the lodging house of Margaret Madden. Claiming to be man and wife, they asked the woman for a room and handed her one shilling and sixpence.

Margaret escorted the pair to their room and then returned to her duties. Shortly afterwards, the landlady heard screams of murder. She rushed upstairs and found Mary Ann lying on her side – she was muttering that the man had kicked her; the floor was covered in blood. Medical help was sent for but the victim died before it arrived. Jackson was arrested and tried at the assizes on a charge of manslaughter on 2 December. It took the jury a few minutes to find him guilty, but the sentence was not given until the December Assizes, when the judge declared that Jackson would serve ten years in prison.

8 AUGUST 1903 The body of a married woman named Eliza Range was found murdered at her home. The victim's 13-year-old son Arthur witnessed the tragic events at the family home on Husband Street in Collyhurst. The murderer was named as Charles Wood Whittaker, a labourer, who had been out drinking with Eliza on the day in question.

Shortly before eleven o'clock, Eliza told Whittaker that she needed to leave the house to go and do some cleaning for a Mr White. She then stood up and went into the scullery. Arthur witnessed Whittaker follow his mother into the room with a knife in his hand. In a rage, he stabbed her in the neck and she fell to the floor. Whittaker then fled the scene through the yard. The following day he handed himself in at the police station.

At his trial, it was revealed that Whittaker was having an affair with Eliza and used to frequent the property when Mr Range had left the house. He stated that he had no recollection of the incident, saying that he was extremely drunk at the time. The jury found him guilty of the wilful murder of Eliza and sentenced him to death.

9 AUGUST 1873 On this day, a fatal train accident occurred at the Miles Platting junction. The victim was cotton spinner Charles Newhouse, who lived at Egerton Villa in Heywood.

Newhouse was travelling on the Bury train towards Miles Platting Station when the carriage he was in came off the track and flipped onto its side. Fearing for his life, the spinner jumped from the moving wreckage, hitting the ground and rolling on to his back. Seconds later, another carriage came off the track and landed on top of him, covering the top half of his body. Newhouse was transferred to the Royal Infirmary, where he later died of his injuries.

10 AUGUST 1857 On this day, two men from Manchester were found guilty of bigamy. Henry Lowe, 31, and 26-year-old William Dyson, were both found guilty of marrying women while their first wives were still alive. Lowe, a painter, pleaded guilty and was sentenced to twelve months' imprisonment with hard labour. Dyson, a plasterer, also pleaded guilty and was sentenced to eighteen months' imprisonment.

11 AUGUST 1852 On this day, the families of 17-year-old Thomas Dowd, 29-year-old William Gleave, 52-year-old John Travis and 25-year-old James Farrell were coming to terms with a freak act of nature that had claimed the lives of all four men.

The previous morning, Gleave and Dowd were on their way out when they were caught in a torrential thunderstorm that was battering Manchester, so the pair decided to abort their trip and wait inside a house on Ridgeway Street until it had passed. Once inside the property, they positioned themselves on the windowsill with their backs to the street. Then, shortly before eleven o'clock, a lightning bolt came crashing from the sky and into the window where the two men were sat. The force of the bolt sent the men hurtling into the street. Both Gleave and Dowd were pronounced dead at the scene.

At the same time, two plasterers named John Jones and John Travis were working at the house next door. Jones was fixing moulds and Travis was skimming the kitchen. They were working alongside 25-year-old James Farrell, who was outside mixing plaster.

Jones recalled seeing a flash of light before being knocked out. When he awoke, he discovered that the house had been hit by lightning. Travis had been killed instantly and was found by the window. Farrell was found inside another house with his shirt and left leg on fire. He was also dead, taking the death toll to four.

12 AUGUST 1868 Mr Herford, the coroner for the city of Manchester, held an inquest on the bodies of twenty-three people who had been killed at the Victoria Music Hall. With the exception of a small few, the majority of the victims were under the age of 21. The accident occurred on Friday, 31 July during an evening performance. The performance was very popular; the capacity of the hall was 2,000 people, but on this occasion, the organisers had oversold the show. It was cramped and overcrowded.

The performance began as normal, but midway through, someone in the pit shouted 'Fire!' and the crowd immediately began to panic. In a desperate attempt to escape, people began to jump through the window, while others headed for the nearest staircase. The stone staircase was where the majority of the crowd had chosen to escape and the sheer volume of people resulted in many people being crushed.

A witness described arriving at the scene and seeing a pile of bodies lying on the floor at the base of the stairs. He stated that there were between thirty and forty bodies that were being trampled on by the dispersing crowd. An attempt was made by a number of witnesses to rescue the victims; a number were pronounced dead at the scene, while those that still showed signs of life were sent to the infirmary.

The deceased were named as: William Braxendale; Andrew Battley; Edward Brennan; William Cardwell (16); Caroline Carlisle (11); William Sellars (20); Thomas England (13); John Humphries (15); Sarah Jones (16); John Jennings (14); Joseph Johnson (16); John Charles Keogh (14); Edward Kirby (16); Thomas Long (17); Jerry Malone (20); John McCann (17); James Makin (17); Samuel Poole (20); Edward Price; John Raynolds (15); William Ramsden (16); Elizabeth Strothers (42) and Robert Vanse (16).

After listening to the evidence, the jury returned a verdict of accidental death for all of the victims. In their statement they concluded that the building was not structurally sound and did not have enough fire escapes to accommodate the number of people that were present on the night of the accident. They urged that before any future licenses were granted to music halls or theatres, the Corporation should introduce officials to inspect the premises to ensure that it could accommodate the number of people stated on the license.

13 AUGUST 1851 This week a post-mortem was held on the body of a weaver named James Dooley, who lived with his four sons at No. 15 Front Crescent, Ancoats.

Dooley had committed suicide the previous day by tying a rope to a hook on the roof of his cellar, standing on a wooden chair, placing the rope around his neck and then jumping off the chair. His body was discovered by one of his sons.

At the inquest, his sons revealed that he had been depressed for some time because he was unable to find work. The jury ruled that the deceased man hanged himself while suffering from a period of insanity.

14 AUGUST 1844 On this day, a shocking murder occurred at 40 Bradshaw Street in Hulme. The victim was Jane Millen, who lived at the address with her husband and son. Also residing at the address were two lodgers named Christopher Barningham and George Evans. Evans was a 21-year-old mechanic who worked for John Hetherington & Co., Store Street, Manchester.

Early on this morning, Mrs Millen's husband, son and Barningham left for work, leaving Evans and Mrs Millen in the house. At lunchtime, Mr Millen and Barningham returned to the house to get something to eat. Upon arriving at the house, they found the front door was locked from the inside and there was no response from Mrs Millen.

Mr Millen managed to gain entry by climbing through an open window. Once inside, he opened the door to Barningham and the pair began searching for Mrs Millen. After some time, Barningham opened a small coal storage cupboard under the stairs and discovered the body of Mrs Millen, who was lying face down on the floor. The two men immediately pulled her out and in doing so noticed marks to her head and face. There were also bloodstains on the floor in the kitchen.

One of the men summoned the police, who conducted a full search of the house. The murder weapon appeared to have been a bloodstained, twelve-inch iron bludgeon that was discovered in the kitchen drawer and it was concluded that the motive had been robbery. Missing from the house was a sum of money, three suits, sugar tongs, teaspoons and a silver watch. The main suspect was reported as lodger George Evans, who had remained in the house after the other men had left for work.

A neighbour by the name of Sarah Beswick reported seeing a hackney coach pull up outside the house shortly before ten o'clock. She just had time to notice Evans climb inside before the coach drove off. The driver of the coach later stated that he gave Evans a lift to the Liverpool and Manchester railway station on Liverpool Road, where he was to board a train to Liverpool.

The following morning, Liverpool officers tracked the accused down to a lodging house near the Clarence Dock. In his possession were a number of the stolen items. George Evans was put on the first available train back to Manchester and transferred to the Chorlton-upon-Medlock station, were he remained until appearance at the Borough Court.

Evan's trial was held on 9 December 1844. After hearing the evidence, the jury found him guilty of murder and he was sentenced to death. He was executed on 4 January 1845 at Kirkdale.

15 AUGUST 1875 On this day, two 12-year-old boys named John Southart and Edward Withington drowned while swimming at the Cottage Pits in Moss Side. Shortly after three o'clock in the afternoon, the two lads and a group of friends arrived at the pits to have a swim. The lads were playing in the water when Southart got into difficulty. Upon seeing that his friend was in trouble, Withington swam over and attempted to rescue him. When he eventually reached Southart, the weight of his clothes began to drag him under the water. In a desperate bid to save them both, Withington began to take his clothes off, but the pair continued to struggle to keep above the water. Withington began shouting to the other boys stood on the bank to help, but no one came to their rescue. The pair then sank into the water and their bodies were recovered two hours later. The father of John Southart – a man named James, who lived on Argyle Street – identified the body of his son.

16 AUGUST 1819 A crowd of about 60,000 gathered on St Peter's Field to hear a talk by Henry Hunt. The crowd was made up of mostly working-class men,

women and children, who were all there to show their support for democracy and the abolishment of poverty.

Demonstrations were happening across the North West because industrial workers had become disillusioned by the political powers in government and wanted political reform. In the years prior to the meeting, the working classes had faced widespread unemployment and hardship since the introduction of the Corn Laws, which had pushed up the price of bread. The workers also hoped that this rally would improve suffrage across the region, as only around 2 per cent of the whole population were able to vote.

Dressed in their Sunday best, the crowd began gathering in the morning. Shortly after the talk began, worried magistrates began to shout the Riot Act at the crowd. The speakers kept talking and the crowd refused to move. The military – who were already in place – were then called to disperse the crowd and arrest Hunt.

The cavalry came and charged at the unarmed crowd with their swords drawn. Fifteen people were killed and reports suggest that between 500 and 700 people were injured. In a reference to the Battle of Waterloo, the event became known as the Peterloo Massacre.

1851 The *Manchester Courier* reported on the shocking murder of Henry Ellis, who died after being hit over the head with a hammer in an unprovoked attack by a shoemaker named James McNamara.

Four weeks previous, the pair had been drinking together at Ann Oldfield's beerhouse in Queen Street, Hulme, when they got into a quarrel. McNamara then left the beerhouse and returned with a hammer. As Ellis left the premises, McNamara struck him across the head and then fled the scene. Ellis was escorted to his sister's house before being transferred to the infirmary. He then spent the following weeks in and out hospital, finally dying on 10 August as a result of his injuries. McNamara was promptly arrested and his trial was held on 13 August 1851 at the Liverpool Assizes. After listening to the evidence, the jury found him guilty and he was sentenced to twelve months in prison.

17   AUGUST   1866   On this day, the city coroner held an inquest into the death of a young child who had died in a hit-and-run accident. The victim was 17-month-old Ada Chippendale, the daughter of a tobacconist. Shortly after ten o'clock in the evening, Ada was in the arms of her grandmother and the pair were attempting to cross London Road. As they stepped into the road, the driver of a horse and trap that was travelling down the hill shouted at them to get out of the way but he was too close and the cart hit them. The driver failed to slow down or stop; instead he whipped his horse and fled the scene.

The grandmother lay unconscious on the road, with blood coming from her mouth, while the infant was found lying near her body. The woman was transferred to the Royal Infirmary and Ada was taken to her father's house, which was also on London Road. A surgeon was called for, but there was nothing he could do and the child died eight hours later.

After hearing all the evidence, the jury found that the child's death was the result of manslaughter, although the culprit was unknown.

18   AUGUST   1843   Mr and Mrs Kelly appeared at the Borough Court charged with having two gallons of illicit whiskey. The pair were caught after they attempted to sell the alcohol to a druggist in Great Ancoats: Mr Kelly went into the shop and asked the man if he wanted to buy some tobacco, Havana cigars or some fine Irish whiskey. The man said he would buy the whiskey, to which Kelly replied that he would send his wife the following day with the goods. The druggist then informed the excise officer, who lay in wait for the couple the following day.

As promised, Mrs Kelly arrived at the shop the following day with the whiskey. Immediately after entering the premises, she was apprehended. The officers also seized Mr Kelly. After hearing the evidence, the magistrate found Mrs Kelly guilty and fined her £25, stating that if she failed to pay, she would be imprisoned for one month.

Mr Kelly was released without charge because he was not found in possession of the whiskey; however, the magistrate stated that there was no doubt of his guilt.

19 AUGUST 1870 On this day, the *Manchester Guardian* reported the arrest of Patrick Durr for the shocking murder of his wife. Durr was a labourer who lived at No. 1 Court, off Brighton Street, Red Bank, Manchester with his wife Catherine and two children. On the previous Wednesday evening, the couple had been drinking and at about eleven o'clock, they were heard singing. Some time later, an argument broke out. In the struggle, Mr Durr produced a rope with a noose in it, which he put around his wife's neck and pulled as hard as he could until she could not breathe. He then calmly left the room. A short time later he returned and asked his 13-year-old son if she was dead yet. He then walked over to his wife and attempted to pull the rope again whilst leaning on her chest. He did not stop until she was dead.

After he had committed the crime, Durr placed his arm around his son and told him he would be better off without his mother before going to the police station and handing himself in. Paddy, the son, revealed that his mother was not a kind lady; she often pawned their things and spent all of their money, leaving them without any food.

The prisoner was remanded in custody and charged with the murder of his wife. At a later trial he was found guilty and sentenced to death. He was executed shortly after eight o'clock on the morning of 26 December 1870 at Strangeways prison. His execution was only the second in Manchester to be held in private.

As he stepped on to the scaffold, Patrick shouted to the crowd who had gathered outside the prison walls, 'I believe my boys are listening to me outside!' William Calcraft, the executioner, told him he was not permitted to shout to his children, to which he said, 'Oh yes I can. They are listening to me outside'. He then shouted as loud as he could: 'Dear boys, don't fret. This is a debt, to nature due. I must go to the earth that gave me birth, and so must both of you.' He then said, 'Lord Jesus have mercy upon me,' and within a few minutes he had died.

20 AUGUST 1834 A soldier with the Royal Foot Artillery named James Smith, who was residing in the Horse Barracks, Hulme, was apprehended for shooting his wife, Elizabeth.

Elizabeth had previously been married to another soldier and had travelled with him to various postings throughout the world. When the couple were stationed in the West Indies, she disgraced herself and was sent home. Her husband stayed abroad until his service finished and then he returned. Desperate to be rid of Elizabeth, he requested to be posted overseas again, however, on his way he became sick and died.

While he was away, Elizabeth had an affair with James and became pregnant with his child. As she was now a widow, the couple were free to marry, but soon after their wedding they began to drink excessively. Witnesses stated that Mrs Smith would regularly spend all of her husband's wages on drink.

On the day of the murder, James had been drinking in a local beerhouse; he eventually returned home and decided to load his gun. Fearing that he was going to kill himself, Elizabeth ran into the street to get help. As she approached the door to go back inside her house, James fired the gun and shot her in the throat. She staggered and then fell to the floor, dying instantly.

James showed no remorse for his actions and surrendered himself to the authorities immediately. He was sent to trial at the Lancaster Assizes on a charge of wilful murder.

21 AUGUST 1847 The deputy coroner held an inquest this week at the King's Arms pub on Wood Street into the death of a woman named Elizabeth Coutts.

Coutts lived with her son – who was described as 'half witted' – at Higher Temple Street, Chorlton-on-Medlock. The evidence presented to the coroner suggested that the woman had been plagued with mental health problems, pointing to her time in a lunatic asylum.

Coutts's son recalled that two days previous, his mother had been in a state of delirium and refused to go to bed. He eventually persuaded her to sleep, although she refused to go to bed and instead lay on the floor in her clothes. Her son went to bed and was awoken in the middle of the night by his mother, who informed him that she had taken laudanum. She told the boy to go to the local surgeon and get help. Her son went to his house immediately and was told the surgeon would come directly; however, he never came. The surgeon feared that the woman wanted to borrow money, so he did not pay her a visit until the following morning. By the time he arrived it was too late – Coutts had died. After listening to the evidence, the jury ruled that the woman died from taking laudanum whilst in a state of insanity.

22 AUGUST 1876 A dreadful fire broke out in the city on this day, resulting in the loss of three lives. The fire started at eight o'clock in the evening, at the premises of Carson and Moffat, a chemical works situated in Holt Town. The fire brigade raced to the scene and, after half an hour, they managed to gain entry into the building. Once inside they discovered the body of Samuel Carson, who was one of the proprietors of the company. He was 23 years old and lived at St Andrew's Square, Travis Street. Alongside him was the body of a 16-year-old boy by the name of Thomas Pierce. Both corpses were so charred that identifying the two men was near impossible. The men

were discovered facing the door, which led the authorities to believe that they were trying to escape when they died. Another man, who was with Pierce at the time of the fire, managed to escape to safety. He was later transferred to the Manchester Infirmary, where he died of his injuries.

23 **AUGUST** **1891** On this day, tragedy struck the family of a cabinet-maker called George Wallwork. George lived with his wife, four sons and a daughter on Upper Jackson Street, Hulme. Some time after ten o'clock in the evening, three of his sons returned home drunk. Shortly after entering the house, James and Harry Wallwork began arguing. The argument continued in their bedroom and, moments later, James shouted that he had been stabbed. Harry had stabbed him in the chest with a chisel, penetrating his heart and killing him almost instantly. He was later apprehended and sent for trial.

His trial was held on 21 November 1891. He was originally tried for murder, but after hearing the evidence, the charge was reduced to manslaughter and the jury found him guilty. The judge sentenced him to six months in prison.

24 **AUGUST** **1798** George Russell was found guilty of stealing from the bleaching works of Mr Shorrocks. He was sentenced to death and was executed on 15 September, in Newton Health.

An early picture of King Street in 1823 by I. Ralston.

25 AUGUST 1874 On this day, a murder and suicide occurred at the Prince's Club, situated off King Street. The murder victim – Alexander Maclean of Prestwich – was well known in the city. He was a partner in a firm of merchants and commission agents.

At some point in the afternoon, Maclean arrived at the club and took a seat in the room opposite the billiard room. While alone, he began to write a letter to his uncle. Shortly before five o'clock, two brothers named Herbert Thomas Barge and Frederick Barge entered the club. Herbert – who was known as Thomas – seemed agitated and was looking for Maclean. Upon hearing that the commission agent was in the club, he left his brother and went to speak to him. A porter introduced the men and then he left. As he got to the stairs, he heard three gunshots from the room where the men were. Fearing the worst, he ran back to the room, where a shocking scene greeted him: Maclean had been fatally shot. The bullet had entered the man's neck under the left ear and exited through the right side of his jaw. Barge was on the other side of the room with a gunshot wound to the head; clenched in his hand was the gun.

An inquest was held on the bodies the following day at the club. The jury heard the evidence and stated that Maclean was wilfully murdered by Barge. They further remarked that Barge had murdered Mclean while he was insane.

26 AUGUST 1920 An inquest was held on the body of a 46-year-old man named Walter Reed. His body had been discovered in a field adjoining Barlow Moor Road in Chorlton-cum-Hardy.

Reed was born in Doncaster but had been in Manchester to see a woman named Gladys Armfield. He had met Gladys during the war and had formed quite an attachment to her. Three weeks previous, he had declared his love for her, but the feeling was not reciprocated. A couple of days before his death, Gladys saw him, at which point he stated his intention to leave the country. However, he must have had a change of heart and on 17 August he decided to take his own life by drinking poison. Next to his body was a photograph of Gladys. Written across it were the words 'Goodbye dearest, I loved you to the end. It is more than I can bear. Walter.' He also left a book titled *The Girl I Left Behind Me*.

The coroner ruled that the death was caused by suicide, which occurred after Reed drank laudanum.

27 AUGUST 1841 This week, a daring daylight robbery occurred at the premises of Mr Thelwell, St Ann's Square. Thelwell owned a silversmith business that specialised in plates, watches and jewellery. On the previous Sunday, a watchman walked past the shop shortly after eight o' clock in the morning and noted that all was well.

Sometime between ten and eleven o' clock, it is believed that two men entered the shop with false keys, as there was no sign of a break-in, and left with two boxes of goods. The value of the robbery was reported to be in the region of £1,700. The two robbers had stolen a selection of expensive jewellery and some watches.

Some months previous, a similar theft had occurred at the shop – there was no evidence of a break-in and the thieves took plates worth several hundreds of pounds. The perpetrators were never caught.

28 AUGUST 1906 An inquest was held on this day on the body of 18-year-old Martha Jane Watts, who died after drinking poison in an attempted suicide pact with her sweetheart. On the night of 4 August, Martha and her boyfriend John Chapman visited the Junction Theatre in Hulme. Some time in the early hours of the following morning the couple walked to Platt Fields in Rusholme, with the intention of committing suicide together. In their possession was a bottle of poison. After declaring their love for one another, they drank the poison. Martha was immediately affected; she was screaming in pain. John, however, showed no reaction to taking the poison and was able to carry his girlfriend to the house of a woman named Mrs Smith. Smith gave John a mixture of salt and water, which made him sick. The pair tried to get Martha to take the solution in the hope that she too would be sick. However, her lips were so burned that she was unable to take any of the emetic.

Martha and John were later transferred to the Royal Infirmary. John made a full recovery but Martha later died in hospital.

At a later trial, John was found guilty of the murder of Martha Jane Watts. Although the act was mutual, John's survival meant he faced criminal charges. The judge sentenced him to death, but stated that he would make a personal recommendation for his life to be spared. On 21 November, the prisoner received an official reprieve from the Home Office: his sentence was reduced from death by hanging to life imprisonment. The following year his case was reviewed and he was freed from prison but would remain on license.

29 AUGUST 1852 This week an Irish woman travelled from Liverpool to Victoria Station. In her possession was a large trunk, which had been stored at the top of the cabin with other luggage. After the train arrived in Manchester, the trunk was carried off by a porter and handed to the woman, who dragged the box a short distance and undid the locks. She was then seen to open the lid and help out two children. The woman was immediately apprehended and admitted that she had hidden her children in the trunk because she could not afford their fare. The woman was ordered

to pay the children's fare before she was allowed to carry with her journey. If the fare was not paid, the station would keep the trunk as payment.

30 AUGUST 1827 A group of boys appeared at the Lancashire Assizes charged with murdering a youth named Charles Barlow.

On the day of the incident, the boys had skipped Sunday school and gone into some fields. While they were there, some of the group got into an argument, which resulted into a physical fight between 14-year-old Jonathan Brookes and Barlow. Barlow initiated the fight and, spurred on by the other members of the group, it continued for hours. Barlow eventually died of exhaustion.

At a later trial, three of the boys were found guilty of manslaughter: Wiliam Fay and 19-year-old William Adshead was sentenced to three months' hard labour each and Jonathan Brookes was given up to his mother and fined one shilling.

31 AUGUST 1877 Thomas Philips and Alfred Appleby were brought up at the City Police Court charged with obstructing a walkway and with being drunk. The men were part of the 'Joiners Strike' that had gripped the region since April. The men were striking for better pay.

On the previous Thursday, the men were part of a group that were stood on Sherbourne Street, Strangeways. Several police officers spotted the men congregated on the street corner and asked the men to move on, but they refused and a scuffle broke out. Two of the men were then apprehended and taken to the police station.

After the evidence was heard, Appleby was fined five shillings and costs, or he faced seven days' imprisonment. Philips was fined two shillings and sixpence and the judge dismissed the charge of being drunk. The fines were immediately paid to the court and the men were dismissed.

SEPTEMBER

1 SEPTEMBER 1883 Shortly after seven o'clock, a woman named Jane Flynn was seen to be hurrying along the Rochdale Canal with her son James clinging on to her hand. As she reached the bridge, she threw her son into the water before running a few steps ahead and jumping in herself. Thomas Coleman witnessed the incident and, with another man named James Verey, attempted a rescue operation. The men dived into the water and after a struggle, managed to pull Jane out first. They then went back in and brought out her son, who was already dead. Jane was adamant that she wanted to die and fought with her two rescuers to try and get back into the water. She was then taken to the Fairfield Street police station, charged with murder. Her husband stated that she had been acting strangely since their home was broken into and a number of items were stolen. Her husband had tried to make her see a doctor but she refused.

2 SEPTEMBER 1911 On this night, 8-year-old Golda Mosesson was playing with her friends on Waterloo Road in Cheetham when she was hit by a tramcar. Golda was the daughter of a Russian machinist named Alfred Mosesson. The family lived in a two-up two-down terrace house on Pemberton Street, Cheetham.

The tramcar was being driven by Edward Hartley and was travelling to Alexandra Park via Deansgate. As the driver drove along Waterloo Road, he noticed some children playing. The driver sounded his horn to alert them of his presence but, without warning, the young girl ran in front of the tram and fell on to the tracks. The driver was unable to stop the vehicle in time and the tram skidded into Golda. Later that day she sadly succumbed to her injuries.

3 SEPTEMBER 1766 The lunatic asylum opened next to the Royal Infirmary in Daube Holes – now known as Piccadilly. When the hospital opened it could

Manchester Lunatic Asylum.

originally accommodate twenty-two of the city's mentally ill patients. Unlike other asylums at the time, Manchester had separate wings for men, women and divisions within these wings for the different classes. The lunatic asylum was an institution that spread fear and dread among the inhabitants of the city – more than the workhouse. 'The madhouse', as it was often called, had a reputation of ill treatment and cruelty. Patients were often restrained using leather straps or were given ice baths to calm them down. Overall, however, Manchester had a good record for caring for its patients.

In 1847, Manchester Lunatic Hospital moved to a new site in Cheadle, Cheshire. It was believed that the tranquil settings of the new site would speed up the process of recovery.

4 SEPTEMBER 1913 Harry Cragg, the 9-year-old son of a railway porter named Joseph who lived in Birch Street in Gorton, suffered a serious injury whilst riding on the back of a motor car.

On the day in question, the boy was travelling on the back of the car when his foot got caught in the wheel. By the time the vehicle had stopped, his leg had been ripped off at the knee. He was rushed to the Ancoats Hospital but his leg could not be saved.

5 SEPTEMBER 1828 A fatal accident occurred in the vicinity of St John's Street. The victim was 45-year-old married father of five, Lawrence Taylor. He was one of many labourers that had been employed to help deepen the main sewer that ran the length of the street.

All the earth that had been removed from the sewer was piled up at the side of the manhole and Taylor was at the bottom when disaster struck: the pile of earth fell down the manhole, crushing and trapping him underground. It took twenty minutes before his fellow work colleagues were able to remove the earth and rescue Taylor from the sewer, but when the men reached him, it was evident that he was already dead. He was found in the same crouching position that he was in before the accident occurred, with blood coming from his mouth. The body was taken to the Cross Keys pub to await an inquest.

6 SEPTEMBER 1878 On this day, fraudster Leon Lamport was spending his third month in prison after being convicted of conning several men out of hundreds of pounds.

On the surface, Lamport appeared to be a man that could be trusted. He advertised himself as a South African merchant that could get men employment in the Cape of Good Hope for a fee of £150. He even had the appearance of a successful merchant – he wore expensive clothes and had offices in Manchester and Liverpool. However, it was all a front. His offices in Liverpool were barely furnished, with no gas and just a little oil lamp, and his staff had not been paid. When the police searched his properties, they found no evidence of any business in South Africa and Lamport was arrested.

His trial was held in July at the Manchester Assizes. After hearing the evidence, he was found guilty on two counts of fraud and sentenced to fifteen months in prison.

Fraudster Leon Lamport.

7 SEPTEMBER 1849 An inquest was held by the borough coroner, Mr Rutter, on the body of a newborn child. The child was the son of unemployed domestic servant Mary Ann Page.

About four weeks previous, Page arrived at the home of Hannah and Robert Philips, asking if she could lodge with them until she found employment. The couple were unaware of the pregnancy and agreed. Suspicions were only aroused in the week prior to the birth, when Page asked Hannah Philips to collect some herbs for her from a woman who lived in the Bank Top district of Manchester. Page told Philips that the herbs were being used to make a tea, which she would drink to help her get over a cold. When Philips collected the herbs, however, she suspected that they were going to be used to create a miscarriage. After arriving home she confronted Page, who denied that she was pregnant. Not believing her story, Mrs Philips asked her to leave. The desperate woman pleaded with Philips to let her stay one more night, saying that she would find new lodgings in the morning. Philips agreed and Page went to bed.

Throughout the course of the night, Mr and Mrs Philips recalled the woman getting up twice and going to the privy, where she remained for long periods. The last time she left the privy, she asked the couple's son to fetch her some scissors, saying that she needed them to cut a knot.

Fearing something was wrong, Mrs Philips followed her upstairs and asked her what was going on. Page replied that there was something that needed to be cut away. Alarmed, Philips went and fetched some of her neighbours. When they arrived back at the house, they saw Page carrying a bucket of water upstairs, claiming that she was going to clean. Once all the women were in her room, they asked Page if she had given birth and she said she had not. The women then began to search her room and after a short time, one of them found a bonnet box. Upon opening it, she found a bloodstained chemise that was covering the body of a newborn child. The police were immediately called and the child was given to Mr Savage, a local surgeon.

The surgeon revealed that the child had been born alive and healthy, weighing eight pounds. At some point after the birth, the mother had inflicted several stab marks to the face and head, using a pair of scissors. In total the child had six wounds, one of which had penetrated the brain. The jury found the mother guilty of the wilful murder of her child and she was committed for trial at the next Liverpool Assizes.

8 SEPTEMBER 1849 The *Manchester Times* reported on the shocking death of Richard Lilly, who died during a prize fight with a man named John Middleton. The incident occurred on the previous Wednesday when Lilly – who had a reputation in Manchester for being a professional thief – took a fight with Middleton for £2. The fight took place at Throstle Nest, on the bank of the River Irwell. The paper reported that a crowd of over 100 people gathered to watch the fight, which lasted for nearly two hours. John Middleton was eventually declared the winner. Lilly appeared to have died, but after some rubbing, he came around. Brandy was then poured into his mouth but he could not swallow it. A cab was called to take the men to the Northumberland Arms in Streford – which was only a short distance away – but Lilly died on the way. At the inquest, the coroner ruled that all those involved in the fight should be tried for manslaughter.

9 SEPTEMBER 1876 Margaret Dockerty was discovered in her bed with her throat cut. She shared a room with a man named William Flanagan, and both were lodgers at a house on Clarendon Street, Chorlton-on-Medlock.

On the previous day, the couple had been to Manchester Races and had returned home in the evening quite intoxicated. The following morning Flanagan complained to his landlady – a woman called Mrs Kelly – that Dockerty had embarrassed him at the races. Later that afternoon, Mrs Kelly entered Flanagan's room and found Dockerty lying in bed with her throat cut. The woman's clothes were covered in blood and there was also blood on a man's shirt.

Flanagan was arrested and held in custody until his trial. Five days after the body was discovered, the accused man attempted to commit suicide in his cell by cutting his throat with a piece of tin that had contained his food.

138 ✝ A Grim Almanac of Manchester

At a later trial, Flanagan was found guilty of the murder of Margaret Dockerty and was sentenced to death. He was executed at half past eight in the morning on 21 December at Strangeways prison. As he walked to the scaffold, he recited some prayers given to him by the Roman Catholic chaplain. Mr Marwood, the executioner, placed the noose around his neck and adjusted the rope. A white cap was then placed over his head and the man was dropped to his death.

10 SEPTEMBER 1907 A dreadful accident occurred at the works of George Macfarlane & Son, situated on New York Street in Chorlton-on-Medlock. The incident occurred early in the afternoon, when two workers were attempting to move some heavy logs using a crane. The logs were twenty feet in length and weighed up to a ton.

The men had raised one of the logs when it slipped from the crane, crushing the two men that were standing below. No sooner had the first log fallen than two more closely followed, trapping the men under the weight of the timber. The first person to be rescued was 43-year-old married man Peter Green. He was seriously injured and was transferred to the Royal Infirmary, where he later died. The second victim was 23-year-old Arthur O'Donnell. His rescue was more difficult than Green's. By the time his body was found, he was already dead. His head was so badly crushed that his face was unrecognisable. His body was transferred to the mortuary at Cavendish police station until it could be identified.

11 SEPTEMBER 1899 At nine o'clock on this morning, a full passenger train heading for Blackpool was waiting at platform six at Victoria Station. Before it had a chance to depart, a Bury and Radcliffe train entered the station and crashed into the back of the waiting train. The impact crushed the guard's van and damaged two carriages, resulting in twenty-nine people being injured. A makeshift accident room was set up in the station waiting room for those that had minor injuries, while the people that were seriously wounded were transferred to the infirmary. Seven of the injured were kept overnight at the hospital, one of whom was an engineer named Joseph Wilson. Sadly, he later died of his injuries. An inquest and a Board of Trade inquiry found that the accident was caused by a mistake made by one of the two signalmen, who signalled to the Bury train that it was safe to enter the station.

As neither inquiry could prove which man signalled the train, no direct blame could be apportioned.

12 SEPTEMBER 1899 A woman by the name of Mary Carolina Lawless of Pearson Street, Rochdale Road, was sentenced to two months in prison for the

shocking neglect of her four children. It appeared that a few weeks previous, Mary's husband had died. Since his death she had received a considerable sum of money from a number of insurance companies. A witness testified that since receiving the money, Lawless had been on a downward spiral, drinking day and night and not taking care of her children. The prosecution was brought by the NSPCC, who cared for the children after the woman's arrest.

13 SEPTEMBER 1850 An inquest was held this week into the death of 15-month-old George Strahan. George lived with his mother and siblings in the cellar of No. 30 Thompson Street. From seven o'clock in the morning until six o' clock that evening, George's mother went to work at the local oakum shop and he was left in the care of his 10-year-old sister. On the previous Friday, a neighbour had heard screams coming from the cellar where the Strahans lived. When the neighbour entered the cellar, she saw George covered in flames. The neighbour attempted to put out the flames and dress the wounds. When George's mother returned thirty minutes later, she took him to the infirmary, where he died from his injuries. At the inquest it was revealed that George's mother paid 3s a week in rent and only had 2s left to feed herself and five children. The jury ruled that George's death was accidental. The judge criticised the Poor Law commissioners for not providing adequate help for the family, which led to George's mother neglecting her children.

14 SEPTEMBER 1929 At a quarter to seven in the morning, a Mr Chinock arrived at his friend's shop to wake him up. Chinock's friend was a 70-year-old greengrocer named George Cartledge, who resided at a house on Upper Duke Street, Hulme. He had lived alone since the death of his wife some eight months ago. Chinock would call to see his friend every morning and the pair would then walk to the Shudehill market.

On this particular morning, Chinock arrived and found that the front door of the shop was unlocked. Concerned that something was wrong, he entered the premises and discovered Cartledge's lifeless body on the kitchen floor with a rug over his head. He was pronounced dead at the scene. An inquest revealed that the man had died from a fracture to the skull, probably caused by a poker. The victim also had puncture wounds to his hands.

A subsequent police investigation was launched and 40-year-old motor driver John Thomas Mead was arrested and charged with wilful murder. At the beginning of December, he appeared at the Manchester Assizes in a trial that lasted for two days. Mead argued that he had killed the grocer in self-defence. According to his version of events, on the night of 13 September, he saw Cartledge stood at his door and went over to repay him some money that he owed him. The elderly man then invited him into the house. Once inside the kitchen, the pair got into an argument and Mead stated that Cartledge attacked him. In an effort to protect himself, the alleged attacker then picked up a poker and hit the grocer across the head with it.

The jury failed to believe that the crime was one of self-defence and found Mead guilty of manslaughter. The man was then sentenced to penal servitude for fifteen years.

Cartledge was buried on 20 September. His funeral attracted a large group of mourners, who followed the procession to Southern Cemetery. Amongst them was the man's 80-year-old sister, who was escorted away after struggling to watch the proceedings.

15 **SEPTEMBER** 1855 The *Manchester Courier* reported on the shocking murder of William Bell, who was killed while on a night out with his wife in Gorton. On the night in question, Bell, his wife and stepson were leaving the Waggon and Horses pub, when they heard an argument taking place. Bell walked over to try and calm the situation but Michael Healey – an Irishman who was at the heart of the dispute – turned to Bell and, without warning, stabbed him. The attacker's brother, Patrick, then hit Bell across the head with a gutta-percha life preserver (similar to a cosh). Bell died of his injuries.

The inquest revealed that his death was caused by a four-inch stab wound to the abdomen, which had partially divided his small intestine. Witnesses stated that the two brothers threatened to stab any Englishman that went near them. After thirty minutes, the jury ruled that both of the brothers would face a charge of murder. A warrant was issued for their arrest.

Patrick Healey was later arrested and cleared of murder. His brother – who delivered the fatal stab wound – was never caught. It is believed that he fled to America under an assumed name.

16 **SEPTEMBER** 1934 The strike at the wireworks of Richard Johnson & Nephew on Forge Lane, Bradford, entered its third month, with no sign of it being resolved. It was reported that up to 1,000 men had downed tools because of the introduction of the Bedaux system. This new system was supposed to improve productivity by timing the amount of work a person could do per day. If the worker carried out excess work, they would receive extra pay.

Problems arose when employers timed the younger workers, who produced their work at a faster speed then the older workers. This meant that the older workforce found it harder to gain a bonus. Many workers disagreed with this system and it led

The treadmill or treadwheel was used as a form of punishment in many prisons during the nineteenth century. Above is a depiction of a treadmill at a jail in Wicklow, Ireland.

to thousands going on strike across the country which continued throughout the rest of year. At Christmas, relief was offered to those who were still on strike. Over 600 parcels were delivered to striking families. These packages contained a turkey, plum pudding, Christmas cake, oranges, a tin of salmon, two loaves of bread, milk, sugar, tea, carrots, custard, jelly, onions and potatoes. A party was also organised for the children, where they were able to enjoy some entertainment and receive a toy.

17   SEPTEMBER 1830 A man named Adam Rothwell was found guilty of a vicious and unprovoked assault on a stranger. The victim had been drinking in a pub in Gorton where, after becoming intoxicated, he fell asleep, placing his head upon the table. He awoke to find that Rothwell has set his dog on him. When the dog did not bite the victim, Rothwell set about attacking the man, knocking him to the floor and repeatedly kicking him. The attack was delivered with such force that the man swallowed several of his own teeth. The assault was only stopped after a number of bystanders intervened. Rothwell was later found guilty at the New Bailey and given a £5 fine, which he refused to pay. He was therefore sentenced to the treadmill for two months.

18 SEPTEMBER 1830 This was the week that the Duke of Wellington visited Manchester. The duke travelled from Stockport towards Manchester in an open carriage so that he could address the hundreds of well-wishers that lined the streets. When the entourage reached Levenshulme, two 17-year-old boys on horseback joined the convoy. They were scheduled to ride at the side of the carriage, but the driver had not left sufficient room, forcing one of the riders on to the pavement. As the horse mounted the pavement, he lost his footing and fell to the ground, causing the rider to fall off. The duke immediately ordered his carriage to turn around so that he could ensure that the young man was not injured. Luckily, the fallen rider appeared to be in good health. To the surprise of those at the scene, the duke then offered to transport the unfortunate rider to Manchester in his carriage.

19 SEPTEMBER 1853 John Finnigan, 18, was sent to trial for the manslaughter of a 6-year-old boy called James Shanley.

Shanley was deaf and mute. He had been playing with a friend at Bellhouse timber yard when Finnigan pushed him into the Rochdale Canal. Unfortunately the boy could not swim; his drowned body was discovered the following day, thirty yards from where he was pushed in.

On 7 December, Finnigan stood trial at the assizes. He revealed that Shanley had taken a stick from his friend and, filled with rage, he tumbled with the young boy, who fell into the canal. After hearing his version of events, the jury acquitted Finnigan and the boy's death was recorded as an accident.

20 SEPTEMBER 1573 Anyone found to be drunk was to be punished by spending a night in the dungeon. After the drunkard was released, they were ordered to pay sixpence to the poor. If the drunkard was poor, then the owner of the establishment where he or she drank was liable for the money.

1900 Manchester was recovering today after a serious fire damaged the post office and cut off communication to other cities for several hours. The fire started in the telegraph department on the top floor, when a spirit lamp burst into flames.

The whole of the floor was destroyed and the telephone department – which was situated on the floor below – was cleared for several hours while the fire was brought under control. At the time of the blaze, there were 500 telegraphists working and all managed to escape to safety. By the time the fire department arrived, the top floor and the roof were on fire. The men battled for hours to get the fire under control, and two of their number needed hospital treatment after they were hit by falling debris.

Sometime shortly after five o'clock, a connection had been re-established for the stock exchange and communications to London were resumed. By the end of the day, wires were salvaged from the wreck so that the newspaper offices could be connected, but it was not until the following day that the business could began operating normally.

21 SEPTEMBER 1843 At the Borough Court, Samuel Dennis and Richard Rushton were charged with assault and attempting to commit a robbery.

On the evening of 18 September, John Smith had been collecting money for his employer. Smith was an assistant to a grocer named Warburton, who resided on Swan Street. After calling at his last shop, he headed home with a bag containing £30. His route took him up London Road and down Ducie Street. While walking down Ducie Street, Smith felt something hit the wall next to him. Without warning, he was then seized by the accused. One of the attackers placed his hand over Smith's mouth to stop him from shouting while the other wrestled the bag from his hand and then threw him on the floor. Thankfully, a witness saw the attack and gave chase. One of the men was caught on Dale Street and the other was caught in Booth Street.

The men were sentenced to twelve months in prison with hard labour.

22 SEPTEMBER 1872 A man named James Struthers, who resided on Park Street, Hulme, was driving an omnibus when his horses spooked and galloped off. Struthers was employed by the Manchester Carriage Company to take passengers to the races. All was going well that day until he reached Regent Road. As he reached the corner of Cross Lane, the horses fled, trapping him under the vehicle. The man was picked up by a passer-by and taken to Salford Hospital, where it was discovered that he was missing an ear.

23 SEPTEMBER 1907 On this day, a labourer from Ancoats named George Wright was brought up at the City Police Court charged with stabbing James Duffy, who was the landlord of the Queen's Hotel. Wright was drinking in the Queen's Hotel when he thought that someone had stolen his drink. He then asked the landlord to get him another, but Duffy refused and asked him to leave. The young labourer then produced a penknife and stabbed the man in the back. He was later sentenced to six months' imprisonment for his crime.

24 SEPTEMBER 1642 A large army headed by Lord Strange and Lord Richard Molyneux, were en route to Manchester. Known as the Lancashire Royalists, the men were determined to take control of the city from the Parliamentarian force. They had assembled 4,000 foot soldiers, 200 dragoons, 100 light horses and seven cannons.

The men arrived in Manchester the following day and a battle commenced that lasted six days. The Royalists suffered severe casualties and reports suggested they lost over 200 men. In contrast, Manchester lost four of its men. The Royalists later retreated, but in their wake they destroyed many homes and took with them a substantial sum of money.

25 SEPTEMBER 1853 On this day, 55-year-old tailor Hugh Quinn, who lived on Tib Street, left his lodging house and went to visit a friend. Later that evening, a man was walking near the River Irk when he heard cries coming from the river. He spotted a man struggling in the water and rushed to gather some friends in an attempt to save the drowning victim. However, by the time the man was recovered from the water, he was already dead. He was later identified as Hugh Quinn. How he ended up in the water remains a mystery.

26 SEPTEMBER 1906 Sarah Ellis, 52 years old and the wife of Charles Ellis, a furniture broker who lived on Rochdale Road, was crossing Moston Lane when she was knocked down and killed by a cyclist.

27 SEPTEMBER 1876 Herbert Cartledge, a former police officer, was found dead at his home on Rolleston Street. The man's death had occurred because of injuries he had sustained during an attack the previous week.

On Sunday, 17 September, a couple were walking home when they heard cries for help coming from Bank Lane, Clayton. They followed the sounds of the cries and found Herbert lying on his back. Looking at him, it was evident that he had been physically assaulted.

Herbert was helped to his feet and then carried to the local police station. He claimed that he did not see the face of his attacker, but remembered meeting a woman, walking her to Bank Lane and then bidding her goodnight. He then felt a man punch him, which knocked him to the ground. While he was on the floor, two men kicked him and attempted to steal his watch. Herbert then returned home, but never recovered from his injuries.

The jury at the inquest ruled that the man had died as a result of manslaughter, but the attackers were unknown.

Market Street, *c.*1900.

28 SEPTEMBER 1876 On this day, two pickpockets named Charles Smith and Patrick Doolan were brought up at the City Police Court charged with attempting to pick the pockets of Manchester women. Smith had travelled from Newcastle and Doolan had come from Birmingham. A police officer had spotted the men attempting to steal from people on Oldham Street, Market Street and Piccadilly. The men only stopped after they spotted the police officer following them. They were arrested the following day.

Both Doolan and Smith were career criminals: in the past eight years, Smith had spent five years in jail for larceny while Doolan had spent three months in prison in Sutton for stealing a purse, nine months in Stafford for stealing a watch and one month in Chester.

After hearing the evidence, the judge ordered them to hard labour until the trial. The trial was held on 18 October. Both men were found guilty and sentenced to twelve months in prison with hard labour.

29 SEPTEMBER 1922 On this day, 45-year-old housekeeper Gertrude Tinsley was at her place of work when she was violently attacked. Tinsley was sat in front of the fireplace blackening the grate when a man grabbed her from behind and attempted to slit her throat. A violent struggle followed, which left Tinsley with several cuts to

her hands. The man eventually overpowered her and cut her neck so badly that her head was nearly completely severed. The woman died before her body was found.

Neighbours stated that they saw a man leave the house and believed it to be Gertrude's estranged husband, Arthur Tinsley. Immediately the police issued a description of the man, stating that he was wanted on suspicion of murder.

The search for him ended the following day, when he was discovered hanging in a stable at Hough End Hall Farm, Chorlton-upon-Medlock. The man had committed suicide by hanging himself from a loft ladder. In his pocket was a note that read 'I have done a terrible deed'. The death of Arthur and Gertrude meant that their four children were now orphans.

30 SEPTEMBER 1889 An inquest was held on this day on the body of 31-year-old James Grant. He was recorded as leaving for work on the previous Friday morning shortly before six o'clock. He was employed as a ballast man by the Lancashire and Yorkshire Railway Company.

Later that day, Grant and five other employees began drinking brandy in the platelayer's cabin near Miles Platting. The men had got the alcohol from a broken cask that was on one of the waggons. The cask contained thirty-six gallons and only eighteen could be accounted for, estimating that the men had got through the remaining eighteen gallons.

By half past five, two of the men were severely intoxicated. Grant, meanwhile, appeared to be struggling for breath and was barely conscious. A doctor was called but the man died. At the inquest, the jury ruled that alcohol poisoning caused his death.

OCTOBER

1 OCTOBER 1881 Charlotte Barton, a prisoner from Manchester, was sat in her cell reading a letter from her father Thomas Pimlett. From 1880 to 1883, Charlotte wrote over ten letters to her father, who lived on Allen Street, Greenhayes. Pimlett was illiterate, so his granddaughter replied to all of his letters on his behalf.

Charlotte had been imprisoned since 18 October 1880. She was convicted of stealing a piece of clothing from a man named William Bush and sentenced to five years' penal servitude, with seven years under police supervision. She was described as being five feet tall, with a fair complexion, brown hair, blue eyes, a stout build and an oval face. She also had a scar on the left side of her forehead.

After being admitted to Strangeways prison in 1880, Barton was moved between Millbank Prison, Fulham Prison and the Russell House Refuge before eventually being released on 22 February 1884. During her time in prison she was employed in knitting, picking cotton wool, and in the laundry room; she was punished twice for singing in her cell during the silence of breakfast hour and dinner hour and she received no visitors during her three-year stay.

This was not the first time Charlotte had been in prison and it would not be the last. In 1877, she had been imprisoned on two occasions for stealing. The year after her release, she was back inside for being drunk and riotous. Barton also had ten convictions for prostitution and drunkenness.

2 OCTOBER 1907 Four electricians were working in a lift at the Midland Hotel when a terrible accident occurred. The men were in the lift and had planned to stop at the floor above. Upon reaching their destination, one of the men attempted to stop

the lift, but it kept on going up. He managed to stop it at the next floor and step out but, on turning around, he noticed that the lift was continuing its ascent.

An 18-year-old electrician named George Dewse attempted to escape by climbing on top of the lift. As he put his head out of the cage, he failed to notice that the lift had reached the top of the shaft. His head was crushed and he died instantly.

The Midland Hotel, c.1900.

3 OCTOBER 1900 On this day, an attendant at the Crumpsall Workhouse callously murdered one of his patients. The victim was a man named Francis Southgate, who had learning difficulties and had resided in the workhouse since the previous April, when he was admitted to the 'imbecelle' ward suffering from paralysis.

On the night in question, the victim was lying in his bed, making loud noises. George Prescott, the attendant on duty, approached Southgate and told him to stop making a noise. Then, Prescott suddenly lost his temper, pulled Southgate out of his bed and began strangling him on the floor. Another attendant named Tattersall even held the legs of the victim so he could not move, and the abuse continued. After twenty minutes, the attack was eventually stopped by another man identified as Hurst. The inmate then crawled back into bed.

Southgate continued to make noises and was restrained twice more during the evening. The final time was shortly after three o'clock in the morning. Prescott again demanded that he stop and when his threats failed, ordered Tattersall to fetch a towel and a poker. The attendant then tied the towel around Southgate's neck and began twisting it with the poker until the victim stopped breathing. The attendant then put the body in bed and threatened Tattersall not to speak about what had occurred. The following morning, however, Tattersall and two other men reported the crime to the workhouse master and Prescott was arrested.

At the trial he claimed that the pressure of looking after over 100 patients had caused him to lose his temper. The judge dismissed this, stating that the attendant should have got help to restrain the man using the proper measures. The man was found guilty of manslaughter and sentenced to seven years' penal servitude.

4 OCTOBER 1890 A Corporation worker named William Squirrel, his wife Sarah Ann Squirrel, and two of his children were in the kitchen of his home on Stockport Road, Levenshulme on this day. Just after noon, one of the neighbours reported hearing a gunshot. They rushed into the house and discovered Mrs Squirrel slumped in a chair, with a gunshot wound to her face. According to the couple's son, William was cleaning his gun when, without warning, he turned and fired it at his wife. William was a keen shooter and kept his guns hung up in the house.

At the inquest, the 15-year-old stepson of Mr Squirrel stated the couple regularly argued because he was having an affair with a neighbour. He also said that his stepfather regularly beat his mother and that she was not allowed to sleep in his bed. The jury found him guilty of wilful murder and sent him for trial at the next Manchester Assizes.

The trial was held on 28 November, when Squirrel's defence argued that the woman's death was an accident. However, this was not the opinion of Mr Squirrel's 7-year-old son, who stated that his father intentionally fired at his mother. In summing up, the judge dismissed the children's statements and stated that there was no argument for murder. The jury then returned a verdict of not guilty and the man was released.

5 OCTOBER 1737 This week, John Leadbeater and Mary Dunbar were fined twenty shillings each for lodging and harbouring strollers and strangers.

6 OCTOBER 1902 Manchester thief Jonas Sumner was committed to prison for two months. On this occasion, he had been found guilty of stealing two chisels. Between 1901 and 1909, Sumner was convicted twice for stealing lead, shop breaking and assaulting a police officer. Sumner, just 16 years old, was described as being five feet four inches tall, with brown hair, brown eyes and a dark complexion.

7 OCTOBER 1885 On this day, a woman named Kate Hines was assaulted as she walked across a field in Cheetham Hill. The attacker was a 42-year-old factory operative named Lawrence Flynn.

On the morning of the attack, Hines was released from the workhouse. Waiting outside the gates for her was Lawrence Flynn. He walked with her some distance and then began shouting at her for going into the workhouse and leaving him with nothing in the house. Flynn then produced an iron bar and began hitting her. Hines received thirteen injuries, with seven being of a serious nature. She was transferred to the infirmary and Flynn was apprehended.

At a later trial, the jury found Flynn guilty of causing grievous bodily harm and sentenced him to eighteen months' imprisonment with hard labour.

8 OCTOBER 1767 Manchester experienced one of the worst floods in its history. Heavy rain caused the rivers Irwell and Mersey to burst their banks, flooding several fields. Large quantities of hay and corn were swept away with the current, while goods were also damaged at Salford Quays. It was estimated that the cost of the floods would run to several hundred pounds.

9 OCTOBER 1855 John Percival, beerhouse keeper, was found guilty of assaulting a servant named Jane Swarbrick. It appeared that the previous Saturday, Percival came home drunk and asked the girl to leave the house. Swarbrick stated she would not leave without her wages and, enraged, the defendant then hit her, knocking her to the floor. He was found guilty and ordered to pay forty shillings and costs.

10 OCTOBER 1855 A man named James Edge was working at a gas station on Every Street in Ancoats when he slipped and fell into a gasholder filled with water and drowned. Witnesses stated that on the morning of the accident, the victim was spotted attempting to get out of the pit through a manhole. However, when the man never surfaced, an alarm was raised and he was reported missing. It was believed that Edge – who could not swim – must have fallen into the holder and drowned. For two days, men searched the gasholder and eventually discovered his body.

11 OCTOBER 1918 On this day, the police were called to a house on Rosebery Street, Ardwick, where they discovered the body of a 22-month-old infant. Next to the body was a note from the mother, an unmarried woman named Leah Shanley. The mother stated that she had murdered the child and was about to take her own life, because she was heartbroken and could not carry on. She went on to say that she loved her son too much to leave him behind.

At the inquest it was revealed that the infant died from a morphine overdose. Leah's body was found several weeks later. She had indeed taken her own life.

12 OCTOBER 1905 An organ builder named Giovanni DeMatteis, and a hawker named William Green, got into a fight on Great Ancoats Street. DeMatteis, Green, and a group of other men had spent the day drinking at the Queen Adelaide public house. The men left at closing time and shortly after, words were exchanged and the pair starting fighting. A couple of punches were thrown and Green fell to the floor. DeMatteis then climbed onto some railings. Green managed to get back to his feet and attempted to charge at the organ builder. DeMatteis fell off the railings and bumped into Green, who fell on the floor again. This time he did not get up. Green was transferred to the infirmary, where he died of aseptic meningitis.

At a later trial at the assizes, the jury found DeMatteis guilty of manslaughter, but recommended that he be treated mercifully by the judge. The judge sentenced him to three days' imprisonment and because of time served, he was at once discharged.

13 OCTOBER 1924 Councillor Thomas Hewlett and his two sons were travelling by car to Manchester from their home in Northenden. Councillor Hewlett was sat in the passenger seat, his eldest son Thomas was driving and his 32-year-old son Horace was sat on the back seat behind his father. The party was travelling along Wilmslow Road at approximately eighteen miles per hour. At the same time, a young girl riding a bicycle was coming out of Egerton Road and rode into the path of an oncoming vehicle. Upon seeing the girl, the driver swerved and skidded to miss a collision, but instead collided with the councillor's car.

The car hit the Hewletts' vehicle between the door and the right axle. The impact smashed the door window and a shard of glass went into Horace's neck. Councillor Hewlett rushed to the aid of his son and placed his hand over the wound in an attempted to stop the bleeding. Horace was then helped to the surgery of a doctor who battled to save his life before being transferred to the infirmary, where he died the same day of his injuries.

14 OCTOBER 1899 A fire broke out in the kitchen of a house on Caroline Street, Hulme and resulted in the deaths of two women, Elizabeth Taylor and her 15-year-old daughter Lily, who were fast asleep in a room above. The fire department arrived shortly after the blaze was discovered and the men attempted to rescue the occupants. The bodies of the two women were later found in the bedroom. Elizabeth was still in bed; Lily, meanwhile, had attempted to hide under the bed and had become trapped. The inquest was held two days later and it was ruled that both of the deaths were accidental.

15 OCTOBER 1837 This week several newspapers reported on the murder of Jonathan Fielding, governor of the Prestwich Workhouse.

The incident had occurred on 4 September. The murderer was a man named Joseph Dennerley, who had been admitted to the workhouse with his family some months previous. Dennerley objected to the rules of the workhouse and regularly came and went as he pleased – an attitude that led to clashes with the governor and staff.

On the day of the attack, Fielding was in the day room talking to some inmates when Dennerley entered, carrying a weaver's drying iron. He calmly placed the iron into the fire and kept it there until it was hot. Without warning, Dennerley then hit the governor across the face with the iron twice, knocking him to the floor. The governor was transferred to his bed, where he remained for the next five weeks until his death. The prisoner was later arrested and sent to the assizes.

The trial was held on 30 March 1838. After hearing all the evidence, the jury found the prisoner not guilty on the grounds that he was insane at the time of the act. The verdict came as a shock to the local media, which pointed out that there was nothing in the evidence to suggest the man was insane.

16 OCTOBER 1876 At the City Police Court today, a brushmaker named John Milan was charged with partaking in a prizefight near Philip's Park. Milan, who lived in a court off Angel Street, was caught in the midst of the fight by two police officers, but his opponent managed to escape. The two men had been fighting for stakes of £5 each. By the time the fight started there was said to be a crowd of over 300 people, most of whom quickly dispersed at the sight of the police. Milan was found guilty of a public order offence and was ordered to keep the peace for six months.

17 OCTOBER 1855 An inquest was held on the body of 6-week-old Maria Johnson, the daughter of James and Mary Johnson who lived on Crossley Street. Maria and her twin sister had been suffering with a bowel complaint, so to help alleviate the symptoms, Mrs Johnson gave the girls some 'poppy tea'.

The tea was recommended by a woman named Mary Gossilton, who was the keeper of a provision shop. Mrs Johnson had gone to her for advice after medicine that had been prescribed by the doctor at the homeopathic dispensary did not work.

Mrs Johnson gave the girls the tea in the evening and then put them to bed. The following morning, one of the girls woke up at the usual time, but Maria was still asleep. After seeking advice from a neighbour, Mrs Johnson left her daughter to sleep until the following morning, when she called for a doctor. By the time the doctor arrived, the child was already dead. The cause of death was returned as an overdose of syrup of poppies.

18 OCTOBER 1836 Elizabeth Todd was burnt to death at a beerhouse on Oak Street. She had been drinking the previous evening and, while intoxicated, she attempted to light a fire, managing to set her dress on fire in the process. A woman identified only as Jackson – who also resided at the house – heard her screams and came rushing to the kitchen. Todd was lying on the floor. Her body was charred and her features were so burnt that she was unrecognisable. An inquest was held the following day and the jury concluded that the death was 'accidental'.

19 OCTOBER 1839 On this day Catherine Ainsworth, who resided in Fennel Street, went to Shudehill to purchase two hens. After paying for her poultry, she had half a sovereign and thirty shillings in her purse. As she wove her way through the busy market, she was accosted by a group of men who were trying to entice her to buy some goods. One of the men was named as 20-year-old Henry Schofield. He and his associates were well known to the police as persistent thieves, who regularly operated in the area of Shudehill.

Later that day, Ainsworth checked her pockets and found that her purse had been stolen. A witness – who was with the woman at the time – stated that he saw one of Schofield's gang bump into her, and later observed him counting some money from a purse in an alley. The police took Schofield into custody and charged him with pickpocketing. He was then committed for trial. After hearing the evidence, the jury acquitted him on the grounds that there was not enough evidence to prove his guilt. No one was ever found guilty of the theft.

1946 Olive Balchin was tragically battered with a hammer and left for dead on the site of the Manchester Blitz. Her body was discovered the following day just off Deansgate. Alongside the woman's body was a leather beater's hammer that weighed two pounds. The identity of the killer was a mystery.

After a police enquiry, however, two witnesses came forward to state that they had seen Olive arguing with a man called William Graham Rowland. He was later arrested and his clothes were sent to a forensic science laboratory in Preston. Tests revealed that substances present at the murder scene were also present inside the turn-up of Rowland's trousers. A stain of blood was also discovered on one of the man's shoes.

Rowland's trial at the Manchester Assizes began on 12 December. The jury sat through all the evidence – including a man who testified that he sold the hammer to the accused – and found him guilty. The judge then sentenced him to death. The defendant attempted to appeal the sentence, but he was refused.

Rowland was executed on 27 February 1947 at Strangeways prison. It was later revealed that this was not the first time that Rowland had committed a murder. In 1934, he was convicted of strangling his daughter and sentenced to life imprisonment; however, he was released eight years into his sentence to serve in the war effort.

20 OCTOBER 1877 A group of girls were eating some sweets on Salter Street, when a gang of boys walked over and attempted to steal the sweets. Sarah Ellen Mack managed to keep hold of them, stopping a 16-year-old lad named Harry Campbell from taking them. Furious, Campbell grabbed the girl's shawl and ran off. Sometime later he returned and offered to give the girl her shawl back. As she went to grab it, Campbell fired a shot into her face. Sarah was taken to the Ancoats dispensary, where she stayed for two weeks. Campbell was later arrested and admitted to throwing the gun in the Ashton Canal. Later that year he was ordered to appear at the sessions. After hearing the evidence, the case was thrown out of court by the jury.

21 OCTOBER 1856 On this day, a young Irish mother named Bridget Kelly murdered her child.

Some time in the morning, Kelly discharged herself from the workhouse, saying that she was going to live with a relative in Birmingham. However, the story was a lie and she spent the next few hours roaming the local fields with her child looking for work and a place to stay. Around six o'clock, she made the horrific decision to murder her child by throwing it into the canal near Mill Street, Ancoats. The body was discovered the following Saturday. A woman from the workhouse identified the child by its socks.

Kelly was later arrested and confessed to the murder. A post-mortem revealed that the child died from drowning. Kelly was sent to the assizes on a charge of murder, found guilty and sentenced to death by hanging.

22 OCTOBER 1889 The residents of Didsbury were coming to terms with a daring theft which resulted in one man being seriously injured and another being killed.

The events began in the morning, at the Union Bank. At half past nine Harold Cuppleditch, a junior clerk, and manager Richard Allen opened up the bank as usual. Shortly after ten o'clock Joseph Dwyer – a former porter at the Carlton Club – walked into the bank, claiming he wanted to deposit a large sum of money. Without warning, he then produced a gun and shot Allen. With the manager on the floor, Dwyer jumped over the counter and began to rob the bank, stealing £78. Allen and Cuppleditch managed to make their escape through a back door and, once outside, they noticed the thief walking up Wilmslow Road in the direction of the station. The clerk gave chase but lost him at the corner of North Street. Dwyer was next spotted attempting to hide in the garden of Parkfield, a house owned by a Mr Hampson. Two gardeners that were emptying manure onto the compost heap spotted the man in the garden. Dwyer threatened to shoot the pair but he could not get his gun out of his pocket, so he fled. He had only gone a short distance when he managed to free his gun and started to fire at the gardeners, who were now giving chase. Dwyer fled through the fields at the back of the house and then jumped a fence onto Parkfield Road. Realising that he was surrounded, he pointed the gun in his mouth and pulled the trigger. He died almost instantly. The body was placed inside the Wellington Hotel, Didsbury until the inquest.

The initial motive for the robbery was unclear, as it appeared that the deceased man was not short of money. He lived in a nice house and received sixpence per day as a reserve in the army; until shortly before committing the crime, he was also in employment. However, further investigation revealed that Dwyer liked to bet, running up debts of £130. The inquest also heard that the deceased had suffered with severe mental health problems since leaving the army, often threatening to kill himself.

23 OCTOBER 1877 A widow named Elizabeth Coleman was gravely ill, having recently suffered a miscarriage. The illness was unexpected; the miscarriage, however, was not.

In early October, Elizabeth visited a former midwife named Ann Cartledge. Coleman had asked the elderly midwife to perform an abortion, which was illegal in Victorian England. The women met several times in a house on Rex Street and the abortion took place on Sunday, 21 October. The following day, Coleman began vomiting and suffering from peritonitis, an infection in the thin layer of tissue that lines the stomach. Coleman died the morning after the miscarriage.

Cartledge was later arrested and sent to the next assizes for trial, which took place on 12 November. The elderly woman was found guilty of the murder of Elizabeth Coleman and sentenced to death. She was later spared the gallows on account of her age.

24 OCTOBER 1853 On this day, an inquest was held into the death of 4-year-old William Shape. The young boy was sat on a trunk at the side of the river at Castlefield when he fell into the water. His father – who was with the boy at the time of the accident – had only turned his back for a minute when his son went missing. The frantic father searched the river and some time later the boy's body was discovered. The cause of death was ruled as drowning.

25 OCTOBER 1913 A man named James Edward Dolan was stabbed after getting involved in a quarrel with a mystery Irishman. The incident occurred at a lodging house on Crown Lane, which was in the district of Corporation Street. The attacker was described as being between 33 and 35 years old, five foot eight or nine inches, with a sandy moustache and a fresh complexion with scars on his face. He was wearing cord trousers and a cap and muffler.

26 OCTOBER 1914 Nellie Galloway, 18, was on her way home after doing some shopping with her sister when she was attacked. The two girls and a man named

Henry Brown were walking along Temperance Street in Ardwick when Brown put his arm around Nellie's neck. Without warning, he produced a razor and slit her throat. He then fled the scene. Nellie died on the way to the infirmary and the post-mortem revealed that the young woman died from a haemorrhage caused by the wound. Brown was caught the following day hiding in an empty railway carriage at Old Trafford. He was found to be carrying a bloodstained razor.

The inquest heard that 19-year-old Brown had been dating the girl for some years. Since his father had thrown him out, he had been lodging with the Galloways at their home. The relationship between Brown and Galloway was a precarious one; the couple regularly argued and Nellie Galloway and her mother had recently told Brown that he should go back home and live with his parents.

At the trial, he was found guilty of the murder of Nellie Galloway and sentenced to death. After a successful appeal, his sentence was reduced to life imprisonment.

27 OCTOBER 1853 On this day, 4-month-old Louisa Thompson died after succumbing to injuries that she had received on 27 July. On the day of the incident, the young child was in the care of her mother at the family home on Saville Street. Some time in the morning, the mother left the house and was gone for about ten minutes. She had shut the back door but not the front and, upon returning, she noticed the neighbour's son – a five-year-old boy named John Burke – leaving the house.

Mrs Thompson entered her home and found her daughter screaming. The little girl had black around her mouth, so she was immediately taken to the dispensary and it was confirmed that the black marks were burns. Mrs Thompson questioned the neighbour's child, who stated that he had heard the infant crying and decided to put the poker in her mouth. Louisa died three months later of her injuries.

At the inquest, the jury found that the child had died by burns inflicted by the young John Burke.

28 OCTOBER 1896 A group of theatre workers were playing cards at their lodging house on Wilton Street, off Oxford Road, when an argument broke out between two actresses named Rosetta Burrows and Minnie Beatrice Manderson. The argument quickly progressed into a physical fight and in the struggle a paraffin lamp fell onto Manderson, burning her severely. She later died in the infirmary. Burrows was later arrested on suspicion of murder, accused of throwing the lamp at Manderson. The jury at the inquest reduced the crime to manslaughter and Burrows was then sent to court for trial. The jury at the assizes found Burrows not guilty and she was released from prison.

29 OCTOBER 1909 At around midnight, Mary Scatterwood was found with her clothes on fire. The lady was at her home on Severn Street, Deansgate when she set herself on fire. Neighbours tried in vain to extinguish the flames but the lady died on the way to the Royal Infirmary.

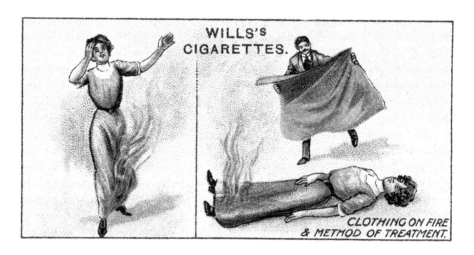

30 OCTOBER 1829 Jane Cummins, a 21-year-old prostitute, was working at a brothel on Spear Street when she mysteriously dropped down dead. The girl had begun her shift the previous evening and at some point in the early hours of the morning she went to bed with an old man and another gentleman. At four o'clock in the morning it was discovered that she had died. An inquest was conducted the following day and it was revealed that the woman had died from a heart complaint and nothing untoward had taken place.

31 OCTOBER 1834 Mary Turner, the 11-year-old daughter of a dyer, burned to death in her home. Mary lived with her parents in the cellar of a house on Mayor Street, which was in the St George's Road district of Manchester.

The event occurred early on Friday morning, shortly after Mary's mother had left the house. About eight o'clock, the young girl was holding her sister in her arms and trying to light straws by the fire, when one of the flames caught her dress. Mary's dress was quickly engulfed in flames. She threw her sister on the bed and ran into the street screaming for help, at which point a neighbour came to her rescue by taking off her apron and wrapping it around the girl to extinguish the flames. Mary was then taken to the infirmary, where she remained for a week; however, she later died at home. The jury at her inquest returned a verdict of accidental death.

NOVEMBER

1 NOVEMBER 1876 This week an inquest was held at the Old Cock Inn in Didsbury into the cause of death of Sarah and Charles Hallbrook. Sarah was the wife of gardener William Hallbrook, who lived in Didsbury. Charles was their 4-year-old son. Mrs Hallbrook liked a drink and while under the influence would often threaten to kill the children with a poker, if she was refused money from her husband.

On the previous Saturday evening, the woman had taken the boy out of the house for a walk. She was spotted walking away from Barlow Moor and heading towards Northenden Lane. The witness then stated that the woman walked towards the bank of the River Mersey and threw herself and the child into the canal. The bodies were discovered the following day wrapped in each other's arms.

The jury ruled that Sarah had committed suicide, but had wilfully murdered her child.

The Old Cock Inn, Didsbury, c.1900.

2 NOVEMBER 1893 Mary Hibbert and Sarah Schofield were sent to the assizes charged with the manslaughter of Mary's 10-month-old child, Elsie Hibbert. The child had been placed in the care of Mrs Schofield while she was at work. The two women lived at a lodging house on Peter Street, which is situated off Pottery Lane in Openshaw. Witnesses stated that the child was regularly left alone, without food or heat, and she appeared skeletal. There were sores on the child's side and her limbs would not straighten because she had been lying in the same position for a long period of time.

Once the authorities had been made aware of the shocking state of the child, she was removed from the mother and sent to the children's shelter. The child died a short time later as a result of being neglected and starved.

The women stood trial on 24 February 1894. Both of them were found guilty of manslaughter and sentenced to 130 days' hard labour.

3 NOVEMBER 1828 Late on this evening, a very wealthy merchant named John Blackwell was walking along Old Cheetham Hill Road when he was set upon by four men. Backwell often worked late and regularly took that route to his home at Crumpsall Hall.

As Blackwell was taking his usual route, he passed the four men, who attempted to make small talk with him. The merchant continued to walk but they seized him. One of the men clamped his hand over Blackwell's mouth so he could not shout. Another man grabbed his arms, while the others attempted ransack his pockets. In the struggle, Blackwell managed to release his right arm and grab his pistol, which was in his pocket. He raised the gun to the stomach of the man in front of him and fired a shot, but the gun misfired and missed the robber. The sound of the gun was enough to scare the thieves, who then fled towards the city centre. The merchant was shaken but unharmed and the only item that was taken was his hat.

4 NOVEMBER 1880 An inquest was held on this day on the body of 41-year-old carter, John Oldfield. Oldfield was employed at Watson & Wagstaffe brewers, Hulme. On the previous Tuesday, he was crossing City Road – in between Alpha Street and Beta Street – when the dray in which he was travelling collided with a tramcar. Oldfield and his horse were knocked to the ground and one of the dray wheels rolled over the head of the victim, killing him instantly. The collision appeared to have been the result of a race between the driver of the tramcar and a driver of an omnibus. The drivers of the two vehicles were brothers. The jury at the inquest ruled a verdict of accidental death and the coroner warned drivers to exercise more caution when using the city's roads.

5 NOVEMBER 1882 This week, a poultry dealer named Michael Allen was sentenced at the assizes to fifteen years' penal servitude for the manslaughter of James Barrow. Allen and Barrow lived in the same court just off Deansgate. It appears that the women in the two families fell out, which led to a deep feud between the warring neighbours. Some time in early August, Allen returned home and found Barrow shouting at his wife and daughter.

A fight then broke out between Allen and Barrow, with the latter giving the most blows. The fight eventually petered out and Allen walked inside his house. While inside, he picked up a poker and then went back into the street, where Barrow was standing. Allen crept up behind him and hit him several times over the head with the poker.

Barrow appeared not to be seriously injured and carried on as normal until 26 August, when he collapsed and died. A post-mortem blamed his death on the blows he received with the poker from Allen.

After hearing the evidence, the jury found him guilty of manslaughter and the judge then passed his sentence of fifteen years' penal servitude.

6 NOVEMBER 1886 This week, a 24-year-old married woman named Margaret McLoughlin was brought up at the assizes charged with concealing the birth of a child. McLoughlin had moved from Dublin to Manchester in September. She made no secrecy of her pregnancy, telling people it was due at Christmas. However, on 14 October, the woman went into labour. Another woman – who was living in the house – noticed that McLoughlin was unwell and went to check on her. Upon seeing the state of her fellow tenant, she went and fetched the doctor, who confirmed that the woman had given birth. They searched the room for the body of the baby but found nothing. Their attention was then alerted to a roaring fire that was in the grate and was quickly extinguished. Inside the grate were some ashes, a small section of the child's foot and some small bones. The woman was then apprehended and taken away by the police.

At her trial, she claimed that she felt a great pain in her stomach, so she decided to take some whiskey. After taking the drink she remembered nothing. The jury listened to the evidence and found her guilty but recommended her for mercy. Upon their recommendation she was sentenced to one month's imprisonment.

7 NOVEMBER 1904 A man named John Shanley appeared at the assizes charged with feloniously wounding a man named James Conway. On 2 September, Conway and a friend were walking along Temple Street when they were approached by Shanley. He immediately began threatening Conway, who retaliated by hitting him and knocking him to the floor. Shanley managed to get up and stabbed him four times with a sharp object in his hand, penetrating the lung. It appeared that the pair had been feuding after Conway had an affair with Shanley's wife.

The injured man was transferred to the infirmary and Shanley was arrested. He was later sentenced to four years' penal servitude for his crime.

8 NOVEMBER 1883 On this day, 63-year-old Ann Davies was brought up at the Manchester Assizes charged with murdering her 5-month-old grandson, Paul Davies. The child's father and his six children had moved into the family home on Lloyd Street after the loss of his wife in June. Also residing at that address were some of his brothers and sisters.

On the morning of the 11th, Ann awoke, got dressed, and walked to the canal with the intention of drowning herself. When she reached the water's edge, she had a change of heart and walked back home. Upon returning to the house, she got the baby out of bed and drowned him in a large bowl of water. She then went and handed herself in to the police.

During her trial at the assizes, her defence team attempted to argue that she was insane at the time the act was committed. Her son Paul further confirmed this by stating that his mother had been in a depressed state since the death of his wife. He also told the jury that an aunt had drowned herself at Matlock and an uncle had tried several times to kill himself.

The jury listened to all the evidence and found the woman guilty of murder, while insane. She was sent to Strangeways, where she was detained as a criminal lunatic until Her Majesty's pleasure should be known.

9 NOVEMBER 1873 Charles Plant died at the infirmary a week after being assaulted. On the previous Sunday, the 39-year-old tailor was drinking rum at the George & Dragon pub. While there he engaged in conversation with a stranger, who asked whom he had voted for at the previous election. Plant said that he had not voted, to which the man asked who would he have voted for if he had and he said 'the Liberals'. Plant carried on drinking in the pub until closing and then left with another tailor named Jonathan Nelson. Nelson walked part of the way and then left the victim to walk the rest of the way alone. Shortly after the pair separated, Plant was attacked and savagely beaten by the 'stranger' whom he had met earlier in the pub. Badly injured, he managed to stagger to his lodgings off Hyde Road. He was discovered the following morning with injuries to face, head and ear and transported to the infirmary, where he died.

At the inquest it was revealed that he died of pneumonia of the right lung, which had been accelerated by the violent attack. The jury ruled that the cause of death was manslaughter by some person unknown.

10 NOVEMBER 1888 On this day Frederick Wright, a fish dealer from Southport, was in Manchester on business. After concluding his affairs in the evening, he decided to go for a drink in the White Lion at Long Millgate. While there, he met two young women named Mary Houghton and Mary Murphy. The women – whose characters were questionable – began working their charms to seduce him. After he appeared quite drunk, the ladies suggested that the group go to another venue. The three of them got into a cab and travelled some distance. The women then asked the driver to pull over while they made a quick stop. Wright and the driver waited in the cab, but the women never returned. Wright then decided to go back to the White Lion. Once back at the pub, he checked the breast pockets of his jacket and found that several banknotes were missing. Wright then summoned the police and the two women were arrested and sent to the sessions for trial. After hearing the evidence, the jury found Mary Murphy guilty and sentenced her to a year's imprisonment. Houghton was acquitted.

11 NOVEMBER 1872 An inquest was held on the bodies of 29-year-old Annie Gurlin and 2-year-old Ada Millicent Gurlin. Annie had been in low spirits since the death of her husband. On the previous Saturday evening, Annie's mother took all her grandchildren, except Ada, to stay with her. The following morning, she returned to the house on Cross Street to drop off the children. After entering the property, she discovered the bodies of her daughter and granddaughter lying on the bed. Both of them were dead.

At a later inquest, a doctor revealed that both deaths were caused by prussic acid. It appears that Annie had murdered her daughter and then drunk the solution herself. After listening to the evidence, the jury stated that the mother poisoned the child before taking her own life.

12 NOVEMBER 1900 A 54-year-old labourer named Henry Thomas Bland appeared at Manchester Assizes charged with the wilful murder of his wife Hannah Bland on 13 July.

Mrs Bland had made her husband a bowl of gruel and had left it on the side to cool down. Then, without warning, Mr Blend stated that he threw the basin at his wife, hitting her on the back of the head. She survived the attack but died three weeks later of the injury. Mr Bland confessed to hitting his wife with the basin; however, after the testimony of an expert medical witness, it was argued that the wound was most likely caused by a hatchet that had been discovered in the house. After listening to the evidence, the judge summed up to the jury, stating that he also doubted the fatal wound could have been caused by a basin being thrown. The jury then retired to consider their verdict. Upon returning to the court, they ruled that the prisoner was guilty of murder but recommended him to mercy. The judge then passed the death sentence.

Later that month, Bland was granted a reprieve and his sentence was reduced to penal servitude for life.

13 NOVEMBER 1874 The body of Hannah Collier, who was found dead at her home on Monsall Street was examined. The 46-year-old woman was the wife of a stonemason named John Collier. A few days previous, Hannah was in Manchester and was pickpocketed of £6. A neighbour visited the house to see how she was and found

her dead on the kitchen floor. She had a cut under her throat and there was a bottle of laudanum on the side. The jury listened to the evidence and ruled that Hannah had committed suicide while of an unsound mind.

14 NOVEMBER 1880 Alfred Hartley, a 40-year-old chemist, was found guilty at the Liverpool Assizes of the manslaughter of a woman named Caroline Barkham.

The shocking events had occurred on the evening of 29 October, when a police officer, who was on duty on Chester Road, Hulme, stopped a man pushing a cart. The man appeared very suspicious and the officer questioned him about the contents of cart, eventually deciding to carry out a search. Under a heap of old rags, the officer made a gruesome discovery: at the bottom of the cart was the body of a woman. The man claimed that the body was that of his wife, and he was taking her home. Not content with his reply, the officer arrested him and took the cart to the local police station. A closer look at the body revealed that she was completely naked and had been beaten around the face.

While in custody, the mystery man refused to answer any questions about how he came to be in possession of the corpse. However, he did give his name as John Smithson, and stated that he was in the employment of a man named Alfred Hartley, who was an oil and drug merchant. The police accompanied Smithson to his address and there they found two people who confirmed that they had prepared the corpse. One of the occupants was a man named Tom Bardsley, who was employed by Hartley, the other was Smithson's wife. Bardsley was arrested on suspicion that he was involved in the woman's murder. Both Bardsley and Smithson's wife protested their innocence, stating that they had got the body from Hartley's shop and were making plans for the woman's burial.

When the police arrived at the shop, they found an apartment with a small bed, which was covered in blood. There were also spots of blood on the walls and some bloodstained clothes were found, which appeared to belong to the victim. Further investigation by the officers revealed that the deceased woman was Hartley's 56-year-old mistress, who resided on Welcomb Street, Hulme. The woman also worked for him as a housekeeper. A warrant was immediately issued for Hartley, who was discovered the following day at the Radnor Hotel enjoying a glass of brandy. The chemist confirmed that the victim had died at his premises on Chester Road, Hulme, and he had asked the men to bury her.

Hartley, Smithson and Bardsley all appeared at the City Police Court on 6 November, charged in connection with the manslaughter of Caroline Barkham. The trial revealed that the woman had died from a disease of the brain; however, marks on her head and face suggested that she had been assaulted. Hartley denied attacking Barkham and stated that he only wanted rid of the body because he was a married man and did not want the shame of another woman being found dead in his shop. He admitted that Barkham had visited him in his shop and the pair had been drinking whiskey together, claiming that when he awoke, the woman was dead. The prisoners were then committed for trial at the Liverpool Assizes.

The trial began on 12 November in front of a packed courtroom and was opened by Mr West QC, who was part of the prosecution team. West detailed the outline of the case, and stated that the deceased had known Hartley for three years. The woman was described as not attractive in her appearance because she had lost the use of an eye during an accident some time before. At the time of her death, it appears that she was living with Hartley, and his wife and children were residing in Southport.

The trial heard from witnesses who were employees of Hartley, who confirmed that he had assaulted Barkham on several occasions. The defence tried to claim that Barkham's injuries were the result of an epileptic fit. The jury took an hour to find Hartley guilty of manslaughter, but acquitted Smithson and Bardsley. The following day, the judge sentenced Alfred Hartley to hard labour for eighteen months.

15 NOVEMBER 1756-7

Widespread food rioting was happening across England. In Manchester, the rioting was concentrated in Shudehill in an incident known as the 'Shudehill Fight'. The rioting was caused by the high price of food. John Bradshaw – who was the High Sheriff of Manchester and the magistrate – gathered an army and dispersed the rioters. During the fighting, four were killed and thirteen were wounded.

1878 An auctioneer named Edward Lawson was released from prison this month, after serving six months for fraud.

Edward Lawson, a Manchester auctioneer convicted of fraud.

16 NOVEMBER 1861 On this day, William Carr and Luke Doyle were awaiting trial after being charged with stabbing two men named Francis Mycock, a porter who lived on Paton Street, and John Trelfa, who ran Trelfa's beerhouse on Granby Row.

The incident had occurred the previous Saturday evening at Trelfa's beerhouse. Trelfa had finished serving beer and was locking up when Doyle, Carr and some other men demanded more alcohol. When the landlord refused, the men began to threaten him, staying that they would stab him. The landlord did not give in, so the men left the building and stood outside. Mycock also left at the same time. When the porter reached the door, Carr ran towards him and without warning stabbed him in his left side. Doyle, who was also brandishing a knife, then ran towards another man, who managed to escape. Doyle then turned to the landlord and slashed him across the face and eye with the knife. Both of the attackers then fled, but were later caught and committed for trial. Carr was sentenced to twelve months' imprisonment and Doyle was sentence to six months.

17 NOVEMBER 1830 An inquest was held on the body of 4-year-old John Horrobin, who died as a result of being murdered by his stepfather Moses Ferneley. The cause of death was listed as sulphuric acid poisoning. Witnesses at the inquest reported that the child had been severely abused by Ferneley; a neighbour stated that she saw the boy being regularly beaten. She said that the child was naked apart from a shirt and was covered in bruises. A former landlady testified that she rented a cellar to the family and often heard the child being physically abused; she even threatened to call the constable. Another witness stated that Ferneley refused to give John food and water. The child appeared to be suffering from a fit when the visitor left the house and died later that afternoon. Fearing something criminal had taken place, a neighbour called the constable and the stepfather was arrested. While in the lock-up, the man admitted to another prisoner that he killed the young boy by poisoning him with vitriol and then finishing him off by kicking and strangling him. The jury found him guilty of the wilful murder of the child and sent him for trial.

His trial was held at Lancaster in March 1831. The jury found him guilty and sentenced him to death. The following Monday – shortly after half past eight – Ferneley and two others were brought to the gallows and hanged. Of the three men, Ferneley took the longest to die. He violently convulsed until he stopped breathing. His body was then removed and transferred to Manchester, where it was passed on to some local surgeons for dissection.

18 NOVEMBER 1896 The occupants of a lodging house on Tiverton Place were in bed when a knock was heard at the door. A cab driver named Arthur Jenkinson Payne answered the door and was met by a man named Samuel Ernest Gibson. Claiming that he had locked himself out of his house, Gibson asked if he could see a fellow lodger named Mrs Robinson. Payne refused, stating that everyone in the house was asleep. The man then left and Payne closed the door. A short time later, another knock was heard at the door. Payne opened it and standing in front of him was Gibson. This time, an argument broke out and the men had a scuffle. In the midst of the fight, Gibson produced a knife and stabbed Payne four times. The injured man then managed to stagger into the house, shouting that he had been stabbed. Gibson was later arrested and sent for trial at the next assizes.

19 NOVEMBER 1906 At this week's assizes, an 18-year-old girl was charged with wilfully murdering her newborn child. The girl had been in service at a house in Cheetham. One day the previous July, she appeared to be very unwell and was confined to her room. Suspicions soon arose that the girl may have been pregnant, so a search of the room was conducted and the body of a child was found in the girl's mail-cart. The child appeared to have died from suffocation because a ball of paper was found stuffed down the baby's throat.

At the trial, the girl denied putting the paper in the child's throat; she stated that she only wiped the baby's mouth with it. The jury found her guilty of the concealment of a child and sentenced her to one month's imprisonment.

20 NOVEMBER 1877 The *Manchester Courier* reported on the attempted murder and suicide of a man and wife who lived off Portland Street. Sometime during the morning, Joseph Smith and his wife Jessie were having an argument. Without warning, Joseph grabbed his wife with one hand and, with his other hand, picked up a knife and slit her throat. With blood gushing from her wound, she managed to break free and run outside. From there she met a policeman who went with her to the infirmary. Another police officer who was passing the house went inside and caught Joseph with a knife attempting to cut his own throat. The officer picked up a chair and threw it at him in the hope it would stop him, but it was too late. Joseph was also transferred to the infirmary but died two hours later from his injuries.

21 NOVEMBER 1829 The *Manchester Guardian* reported on the discovery of a body in the Rochdale Canal, between Union Street and Jersey Street. The body was identified as a Mr Barrett, who had been missing since 23 October. His family had

feared that he had been murdered because he was carrying a considerable amount of money (£79) in his pocket.

It is unclear how the man ended up in the river; one theory is that he was drunk and accidentally fell in. The jury at the inquest ruled that the death was caused by drowning.

22 NOVEMBER 1861-65 During this period, Manchester's cotton workers were facing extreme hardship and poverty as mills across Lancashire closed down because of the Cotton Famine, which lasted from 1861 to 1864.

In Manchester, relief was set up to help those in need. Soup kitchens, fuel, hampers and Christmas meals offered some comfort to the workers. The Corporation gave out-of-work cotton operatives jobs building municipal projects, such as Philip's Park Cemetery.

23 NOVEMBER 1867 On this day, three men named Michael Larkin, Michael O'Brien and William Philip Allen were executed for the murder of a policeman named Sergeant Brett. Larkin, O'Brien and Allan were part of the Irish Republican Brotherhood, a group that was determined to end British rule in Ireland.

The events that led up to the execution began in mid-September, when two men – who were seen in the early hours of the morning loitering near Smithfield Market – were arrested under the Vagrant Act. The two men had Irish-American accents and gave their names as Wright and Williams. It was claimed in the local media that both of them were also carrying loaded weapons. Further investigation revealed that the men were the leaders of the Irish Republican Brotherhood, and their names were Colonel Kelly and Captain Deasey.

On 18 September, the two men were remanded by the magistrate and ordered to be kept at the city gaol (Belle Vue prison) on Hyde Road, Gorton. At some time in the afternoon the men were loaded – along with a group of other criminals – into the prison van and the journey to the gaol began. The van travelled through the city centre, over Ardwick Green and

The headstone of Sergeant Brett.

on to Hyde Road. As the van reached the viaduct of the London and North Western Railway, a series of shots were fired from an open field. The accompanying police left the van and went in search of the gunman. As the men fled, an estimate of thirty to forty Fenians attempted to storm the van. The mob attempted to release the prisoners by breaking in through the roof, but that did not work. Then one of the men fired a shot at the locked door at the same time an officer named Sergeant Charles Brett was peering through the keyhole to see what was going on. The bullet went straight through the man's head and lodged in his hat. He died instantly. With the guard dead, the door was forced open and the two Fenians made their escape.

Several arrests were made after the incident in connection with the murder of Brett, but the two Fenian leaders were not caught – they managed to escape to Liverpool, where they boarded a ship back to New York. After a series of raids throughout the Irish quarters of Manchester, twenty-eight people were apprehended, but only twenty-six were sent for trial.

On 28 October, the trial of the accused began. William Philip Allen, Michael Larkin, Michael O'Brien, Thomas Maguire and Edward O'Meagher Condon were found to be the main perpetrators and their trial was held the following day. All five men were found guilty of the murder of Sergeant Brett and sentenced to death by hanging. However, two of the men would never see the gallows. Maguire's sentence was overturned because the evidence against him was questionable, while Condon was granted a reprieve because he was an American citizen.

The three remaining men were hanged on this day. Thousands gathered at the New Bailey prison, Salford to watch the country's most infamous executioner (William Calcraft) perform his duty. The execution took place shortly after eight o'clock in the morning and Allen died almost instantly, but Larkin and O'Brian had to endure the executioner pulling on their legs to quicken the process.

In the aftermath of the execution, the three men were memorialised in Manchester and in Ireland, earning

A memorial to the Manchester Martyrs in Glasnevin Cemetery, Dublin.

them the name 'Manchester Martyrs'. Monuments were erected in St Joseph's Catholic Cemetery, Moston, and throughout Ireland. Up until recently, a funeral possession with an empty coffin would travel from Dublin centre to the Glasnevin Cemetery, where an empty grave memorialises the men.

Sergeant Brett was buried at the Manchester General Cemetery, Harphurhey. Engraved on his headstone are the words 'Dare Not I must do my duty'. A memorial was also erected on the wall of St Ann's church and a relief fund was set up to provide for his wife and children. His headstone currently lies broken on the ground of the cemetery.

1900 Two women died of arsenic poisoning while at the Crumpsall Workhouse. The women were named as 52-year-old Margaret McCabe and 40-year-old Jane Dyer. The pair had been inmates in the workhouse infirmary since October. At their inquest, it was revealed that both women had been poisoned by arsenic, but how the women administered the poison was unclear.

Margaret McCabe and Jane Dyer were not the only two victims of the mysterious arsenic poisoning; the epidemic had begun in Manchester and Salford in October. By the end of the year, the poison would claim over sixty lives in the North West and would cause suffering to over 6,000 people. When the residents of Manchester first started to experience symptoms of poisoning, the source of the outbreak was unknown. Medical experts examined the victims and concluded that they were all suffering from alcohol-related symptoms and blamed their illness on excessive drinking. It was not until the end of October that it was revealed that the source of the mystery illness was contaminated beer.

Medical experts were sent into Manchester's breweries and found traces of arsenic in the glucose and inverted sugar that was added to the brew. The glucose and inverted sugar had come into the breweries from a sugar refinery named Bostock & Co., which was situated in Garston, Liverpool. The refinery also manufactured sulphuric acid – which contained arsenic. A firm in Leeds had supplied the acid.

Such was the seriousness of the situation that a Royal Commission was ordered the following February. As soon as the source of the poison was confirmed, large numbers of breweries acted immediately to stop further suffering. Across the city, thousands of barrels of beer were poured into the sewers, while anyone caught manufacturing or selling contaminated beer now faced prosecution. Publicans caught selling the old brew could face a fine ranging from twenty shillings to as much as five pounds.

24 NOVEMBER 1891 A groom named Harry Simpson was brought up at the Manchester Assizes charged with breaking into the house of James Bythell. The defendant had entered the house in Levenshulme on 1 October, stealing a coat and three pence in copper. It appeared that the man was in no hurry to leave, as he also helped himself to a hearty meal and a bottle of stout. Two police officers walked in on the hungry thief in the midst of his crime and transferred him to the local lock up.

After hearing all the evidence, the judge sentenced him to fourteen months in prison. This was not the first time Simpson had been to prison: in 1888 he was sentenced to nine months for housebreaking and in 1889 he was sentenced to nine months for receiving stolen property.

25 NOVEMBER 1849 John Hayes, a married father of three, was tragically murdered in Turner Street. The victim had been drinking with some friends in the John Street Tavern beerhouse when they heard the sounds of a woman shouting 'Murder!' coming from the cellar. It was occupied by a bricklayer's assistant named Bernard Sheridan and his wife. The men rushed to the woman and found that she had staggered from the cellar and was lying in the street, with her husband bending over her, giving her a beating. The men managed to get him off his wife and he fled inside. Minutes later, Sheridan returned to the street with a chisel in his hand and attempted to stab one of the men that had helped his wife. John Hayes saw what was going on

and, in order to save his friend, he stood in front of the chisel. Sheridan then drew his hand back and drove the weapon into Hayes. The chisel entered the chest between the sixth and seventh ribs and pierced the heart. The man was transferred to the Royal Infirmary, where he died a short time later.

Bernard Sheridan was found guilty at the next assizes of the wilful murder of John Hayes and was sentenced to transportation for life. On 30 April 1852, Sheridan began his journey to Western Australia on board the prison ship *William Jardine*. The ship arrived on 30 December and Sheridan began his new life.

26 NOVEMBER 1745 Prince Charles Edward Stuart stopped off in Lancashire on his way south with his army as part of the Jacobite uprising. The men arrived in Manchester two days later. They resided in a house on Market Street owned by a Mr Dickinson. While there, Charles mustered a regiment and demanded £5,000 from the city leaders. To ensure they paid the sum, he took an elderly man named James Bayley as a hostage.

27 NOVEMBER 1854 On this day, a cab driver named Peter Threlfall was brought into custody after he was found to be drunk whilst attempting to drive his cab. The police were summoned by a passenger who had been picked up from the Queen's Hotel, Piccadilly. The passenger had instructed Threlfall to take him to London Road Station as he was going to catch the early train to London. Threlfall was so intoxicated that he drove the man down Market Street and kept circling the Royal Exchange, causing him to miss his train. The unfortunate passenger was then stranded in Manchester until late that evening.

Whilst in custody, the driver stated that he had got drunk after consuming a bottle of wine that had been supplied by a previous passenger. Later that day, he was summoned to the City Police Court and found guilty of being drunk and incapable. He was originally fined twenty shillingss, but after refusing to pay it, he was sentenced to twenty-one days in prison.

28 NOVEMBER 1829 A wealthy wholesale dealer named William Marshall violently assaulted two men at his home at Rutland Street, Chorlton Row. Marshall had been drinking and was heavily intoxicated when he invited a watchman back for a drink. When he arrived home, he noticed that his door had been left open. Marshall flew into a rage and began attacking a servant girl who, he claimed, had left the door unlocked. The girl managed to escape and called for the assistance of John Jesse, a local surgeon, and Thomas Gaskell, a watchman. As the two men entered the yard

of the Marshall residence, Mr Marshall ran out of the house and locked the men inside. He then attacked the surgeon with a knife, stabbing him with such force that the blade snapped and stuck in the man's arm. Marshall then let loose two of his fighting dogs, who attacked Gaskell. The dogs savaged the man for several minutes, inflicting over fifty wounds. After the dogs lost interest, Gaskell managed to get himself on a chair. Marshall then approached the victim and hit him across the head before fleeing the house and fetching two other watchmen who offered medical aid to the men and apprehended Marshall. He was then sent to Lancaster Castle where, if found guilty, he faced the death penalty.

His trial took place on 9 March 1830 at the Lancaster Assizes. Marshall claimed that he thought the men were burglars and acted to protect his family and property. The jury believed his story and acquitted him of all charges.

29 NOVEMBER 1895 The body of John Taylor, a hawker who resided in Chapel Street, Levenshulme was examined. Taylor had been arguing with his lodger, a shoemaker named George Duncan, when a scuffle broke out. In the heat of the moment, Duncan – who was cutting tobacco at the time with a knife – stabbed Taylor in the neck, cutting a main artery. Taylor managed to stagger out of his house and was later found dead in the road. He had died from major blood loss.

A jury ruled that George Duncan was guilty of the wilful murder of John Taylor. At a later trial on 27 February 1896, Duncan was found to be insane and it was decided that he was unfit to plead. He was detained in custody at Her Majesty's pleasure.

30 NOVEMBER 1922 A former soldier named James White was found guilty of manslaughter. On 1 September, James and his wife had been drinking at their home in Cheetham. Some time in the evening, the couple's son frantically ran up to a policeman and stated that his father had cut his mother's throat with a knife. The policeman entered the house and found the woman in bed with her throat cut and bleeding heavily. Immediately she was transferred to Ancoats Hospital, where she made a full recovery.

At the City Police Court, Mrs White tried to claim that she cut her throat herself; however, she was not believed and her husband was sent to the assizes for trial. The jury sat through all of the evidence and found him guilty of unlawful wounding. His sentence was deferred.

DECEMBER

1 DECEMBER 1854 A seemingly well-to-do woman named Mary Ann Smith was brought up at the City Police Court charged with picking the pocket of Ellen Hargreaves. Hargreaves had arrived in Manchester on the previous Thursday evening to seek employment as a servant. Whilst collecting her bags, Smith carefully put her hand in the woman's pocket and removed her purse. Smith was then committed for trial at the next sessions, where she was found guilty and sentenced to six months in prison.

2 DECEMBER 1928 On this day, an 11-year-old schoolboy named William Francis O'Donnell was found dead in a secluded field in Chorlton-cum-Hardy.

The tragic events had started the previous day, when the young boy was sent to him room for stealing food from the pantry. Some time later he snuck out of his room and headed towards Chorlton. O'Donnell's family grew concerned when he was not home for dinner. William O'Donnell – father of the deceased – and the victim's brother searched throughout the night in thick fog trying to find the schoolboy.

The following day, a 19-year-old man named Harold Wright was playing golf near to the Jackson's Boat Inn on the banks of the Mersey when he lost his golf ball. After clambering over a wall to retrieve it, he stumbled upon the gruesome discovery of a young boy's dead body. The body was confirmed as William O'Donnell. He had died from a fatal razor wound to the throat. A police officer was immediately called and a murder investigation was launched. Several witnesses came forward stating that they had seen the young lad walking with a man on a bike, but this man was never identified and the boy's killer remains a mystery.

Nine months after the murder, a man serving time in Strangeways claimed to know who killed William. The police continued their investigations but the perpetrator was never caught.

3 DECEMBER 1592 Mr Worsley – keeper of the Manchester gaol – offered to build a workhouse which would provide employment for 'vagabonds, rogues and idlers in the county'. He would build the workhouse at his own expense if he received the 'jail tax' for one whole year.

1919 Ernest Charles Springthorpe, a 23-year-old seaman, was brought up for trial at the Police Court today, charged with intentionally shooting his brother and a man named Mr Boothman on 17 November. The two men were waiting for a tramcar at the junction of Wilmslow Road and Moss Lane East when Springthorpe fired his gun; the bullet hit his brother in the side and went into the knee of Boothman. Both men were treated at the infirmary and made a full recovery.

After hearing all the evidence, the police were satisfied that the shooting was an accident and dropped all the charges against the seaman.

4 DECEMBER 1924 A jury ruled an open verdict on the bodies of 32-year-old Evelyn Higgins and her 7-year-old son Jack. William Higgins, Evelyn's husband, discovered their bodies upon returning home. Mrs Higgins was found on the floor with a slit across her throat and a razor in her hand. Jack was discovered with his head in a tub full of water. With no evidence of foul play, the husband stated that he believed that his son had died by accident while his wife was outside hanging up washing. He then thought that upon returning to the house and discovering that her son had died, Mrs Higgins took a razor and killed herself.

The jury found that there was not enough evidence to state how the young boy got into the water – was it accidental or at the hands of a murderer? They ruled that Mrs Higgins had committed suicide whilst being insane.

5 DECEMBER 1876 On this day, 4-year-old Edward Carey died while at his home on Percival Street. The young boy and his 2-year-old sister had been left alone inside the house while their mother went to see a neighbour. Upon returning an hour later, she discovered that the house was filled with smoke and the young boy was lying on the floor with all of his clothes burnt off. She immediately summoned the doctor, but he could not be saved. He died two days later of his injuries. Edward's sister managed to escape unharmed.

6 DECEMBER 1873 Mary Beswick, a married charwoman with three children, was apprehended for stealing a shawl from a man called Joel Wood. Mary and her husband James Beswick lived in Openshaw.

Mary stood trial for her crime on 12 January 1874 and was sentenced to seven years in prison. It was hoped that the lengthy sentence would pose as a deterrent and stop her from committing crime in the future. Between 1863 and 1874, Mary had received ten convictions for stealing and five summary convictions for drunkenness. During her crime spree she had many different aliases: Mary West, Mary Jones and Alice Bradley. Previously, the longest jail term she had served was twelve months for stealing two blankets.

During her time in prison, her conduct was generally good and she undertook trades such as sewing, knitting and tailoring. She wrote regularly to her husband via a friend, who would read him the letters and reply on his behalf. For her 1874 conviction, Mary served four years and nine months. She was released back to her husband on 16 September 1878.

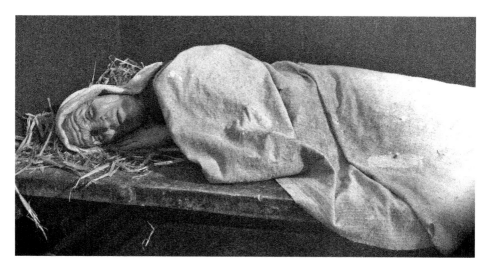

Mary only managed to stay out of trouble for nineteen months. On 26 April 1880, she was sentenced to another seven years for stealing a shawl from James McMullen. By now her family had endured enough of her reoffending: she regularly tried to write to her husband but her letters were returned with 'address unknown'. Her penal record states that she received no visitors during her stay. She was released on 8 January 1886. Her destination was her son's house in Manchester.

7   DECEMBER 1876   Two teenagers – John Callaghan, of Cambridge Street and Thomas Ryan, of Wood Street West – were charged on this day with the murder of Henry John Pennington. Ryan and Callaghan had been playing cards with the brother-in-law of the deceased at the Hadfields beerhouse, Cambridge Street, when an argument broke out over the dealing of the cards. After refusing to play, a scuffle broke out between Pennington's brother-in-law and Thomas Ryan, which ended with the latter and his friends being thrown out of the beerhouse. Once outside, the gang began to cause trouble with the locals, pinning one man by the throat. Anyone that came to disband the group was threatened with a knife.

At about four o'clock in the afternoon, the gang passed No. 3 Charlotte Street, the house of Henry John Pennington. Upon hearing the commotion, Henry went outside to see what was happening. Once outside, he managed to get to the front of the crowd and heard a voice shout that Ryan had attempted to stab a woman. Pennington then grabbed Ryan and began fighting with him. Callaghan came over and gave Pennington a dig in the ribs, at which point he staggered into his house and, once inside, felt blood dripping from his left side. He had been stabbed in between his tenth and eleventh rib and was bleeding profusely. He was admitted to the Royal Infirmary, where he died as a result of complications from the stab wound. Thomas Ryan and John Callaghan were later charged with the wilful murder of Henry John Pennington.

The boys appeared at the assizes on 16 December. After hearing the evidence, the jury found Ryan not guilty and discharged him from the dock. Callaghan was not so lucky, though; the jury found him guilty and the judge passed the sentence of death, but stated that he was appealing for mercy on the grounds of his age. The boy was then taken to his cell while protesting his innocence.

8 DECEMBER 1881 Serial criminal Maria Bell, or Jane Graves (as she was otherwise known) was preparing to spend Christmas in prison after being convicted of breaking into the shop of James Tierney and stealing twenty-two gold rings and a number of brooches. Bell was no stranger to the law. Since she had left her native Ireland, she had received over sixty convictions for prostitution and drunkenness. She had also had four spells in prison for stealing.

On 12 April 1881, she was sentenced to seven years' penal servitude for the robbery at Tierney's shop. During her stay at Her Majesty's pleasure, she was in a constant battle with the other inmates and prison officers. She got into trouble for throwing her dinner over her cell and making a noise during silent time, so as punishment, she had to endure seven days' solitary confinement. On 12 October, she was reprimanded for hiding a pair of scissors. A week later, the convict was told by one of the officers to be quiet during silent time, to which she replied 'she should please herself'. This sort of behaviour carried on for the next two years. In 1883, Bell refused to walk with her fellow inmates during exercise time. She stated that she 'would not walk or talk with any of the women while she was in THAT place'. On one occasion, she even complained to the governor that the chaplain and everyone in the prison were against her because she was Irish.

Bell was released on licence on 18 March 1886. She was put into the care of the Royal Discharged Prisoners Society, which provided her with passage back to Ireland.

9 DECEMBER 1889 This week, one of the worst train crashes in the city's history occurred on the Lancashire and Yorkshire Railway, about half a mile out of Victoria Station. Late on Saturday evening, a freight train pulling seventeen trucks left Victoria Station, heading for Rochdale. Behind the freight train was a passenger train travelling to Bacup. Before the junction of Cheetham Hill, the freight train stopped to let a passenger train go over the junction.

Passing over the junction, the passenger train drove straight into the back of a standing coal train. The wreck spread across the entire track. Some carriages had tumbled off the line and there was coal covering the scene. Two carriages from the passenger train were crumpled – one had travelled up a twenty-foot embankment. The coal carriages were spread in every direction. The scene was one of chaos, with people screaming for help; however, disaster was about to strike again.

Without warning, in the dark of night, a passenger train travelling at approximately thirty miles per hour came tearing around the corner and crashed into the wreckage. The injured were everywhere, and there were screams from people trapped inside the carnage. Miraculously, there was only one fatality.

10 DECEMBER 1901 A man named Henry Palmer was brought up at the City Police Court charged with stabbing an elderly woman named Mary Cornwell on the previous Saturday night at a lodging house on Silk Street. It appeared that the couple had an argument and in the midst of the fight, Palmer reached for a table knife and stabbed the woman in the eye. He was found guilty and sentenced to one month's hard labour.

11 DECEMBER 1908 An inquest was held on the body of a 2-year-old child called Ernest Slater. The young boy had been left unattended at his home on Robert Street in Ardwick when his clothes caught fire. His mother discovered the charred remains of her son when she returned to the house.

The coroner opined that too many children were dying as a result of parents not taking sufficient care against the dangers of open fires. He further stated that in future parents could face prosecution if they failed to provide a fireguard to protect their children.

12 DECEMBER 1874 The body of a man found in the Ashton Canal near Ancoats was examined. The man was named as Alcimus Coulthurst, who lived with his wife and daughter on Chapel Lane in Blackley. Coulthurst worked as a commercial clerk and conducted the majority of his business in Manchester.

On the evening in question, he was last seen at the Wellington Hotel talking to two gentlemen; he appeared slightly drunk and was carrying a travelling case. At about half past nine in the evening, he left the hotel and this was the last time he was seen alive. His body was later found floating in the canal near White Street.

The post-mortem revealed that the man died from a fractured skull, as a result of hitting his head while falling into the water. The jury at the original inquest concluded that the man had been murdered, with the motive being robbery. However, further investigation revealed that none of the man's belongings were missing and the death was ruled as accidental.

13 DECEMBER 1898 On this day, the *Manchester Guardian* reported on a serious tramcar accident that occurred at the junction just off the Stretford Road. The car was travelling along Great Jackson Street when it crossed over Stretford Road and hit a pedestrian. When the car came to a halt, the lady was discovered trapped underneath. She was seriously injured and died shortly after in the infirmary.

14 DECEMBER 1904 Two lovers were tragically shot dead at a house on Merryfield Street. The house was situated just off the Queens Road and was occupied by 57-year-old Margaret Fielding and her three grown-up children, the youngest of whom was called Beatrice Jane. For many years, she had been engaged to a barman called John Fritchley.

On the evening in question, Beatrice arrived home at seven o'clock, with her fiancé following shortly after. Some time later that night, the two got into an argument and Beatrice decided to leave the room. As she stood up, Fritchley pulled out a gun and shot her twice. He then pointed the pistol at his head and pulled the trigger, killing himself instantly. Joseph Livesey – brother-in-law of Beatrice – ran for the doctor, but sadly it was too late and the woman could not be saved.

15 DECEMBER 1876 This week five people were charged with being incorrigible rogues and vagabonds. The charged were named as: 25-year-old Mary Smith; 37-year-old Elizabeth Neary; 25-year-old Ellen Mulligan and 32-year-old Eliza Carroll. All the women were sentenced to twelve months in prison for 'behaving in a riotous and indecent manner in a public street'. The final rogue was named as 33-year-old labourer Jason Robberts. He was charged with absconding from his wife and children, thus leaving them to be provided for by the township of Manchester. For the crime he was sentenced to six months in prison.

16 DECEMBER 1890 The *Manchester Guardian* reported on the unsuccessful attempt to get the Home Secretary to introduce a new law to help deal with 'scuttling'. In a bid to educate the public, the paper had published a series of articles on the subject as, by the end of 1890 in certain parts of Manchester, 'scuttling' had become a real worry for the residents and the police.

In working-class districts, groups of lads had formed gangs and named themselves after roads or areas. These gangs would then meet and 'scuttle' (fight), using weapons. In Manchester and Salford there were the 'Grey Mare Boys' (Grey Mare Lane); 'Ordsal Lane'; 'The Terrace Lads'; 'Holland Street'; 'Bengal Street'; 'The Bungall Boys' (Fairfield district); 'Little Forty' (Hyde Road) and 'Alum Street'. The gangs tended to also have their own unique style of dress, wearing clogs and bell-bottoms. Their hair was also cut short, except for a distinctive long fringe. 'Scuttling' continued to plague Manchester until the turn of the century, when the introduction of new forms of recreation, such as football and social clubs, kept the lads busy.

17 DECEMBER 1830 A young boy was delivering milk in Ardwick Green when he noticed the body of a woman lying on the bank of the pond. The woman appeared to be in her mid-twenties and was dressed in a black silk gown with silk gloves; her bonnet was lying next to her.

The initial identity of the woman was a mystery but eventually a witness at the inquest recognised her as Eliza Anderson, a maid in the service of a Mr Sedgwick, who resided at St Ann's Square. There was no evidence to explain how she had got into the lake and there was no evidence on her body to suggest any foul play. The jury ruled a verdict of found drowned.

18 DECEMBER 1883 A post-mortem was held on the body of Robert Buck Carruthers, who died as a result of a recent storm. Carruthers was a 32-year-old surgeon and chemist who resided in Bradshaw Street, Moss Side.

On the day in question, Carruthers had been visiting a patient by the name of Mr Unsworth, who lived with his wife on Derby Street in the district of Moss Side. The couple were going to bed at eleven o'clock in the evening when a chimney stack fell through the roof, seriously injuring Mrs Unsworth. By the time Carruthers and his wife arrived, Mrs Unsworth was upstairs. While Mr and Mrs Carruthers were bent over the bed attending to the injured woman, a second chimney fell into the room, crushing the occupants under the debris. All three people were pulled out of the rubble alive and transferred to the Royal Infirmary. Mrs Unsworth and Mrs Carruthers made a full recovery and were subsequently discharged. Mr Carruthers survived until the following Sunday, when he died of blood poisoning, which came as a result of gangrene in his leg.

At the inquest, the jury returned a verdict of accidental death. The coroner praised the role of the surgeon who risked his own life to save another and the people of Manchester were so touched by the story that they began a subscription to support the grieving family of the surgeon.

19 DECEMBER 1843 On this day, a 25-year-old man named William Wilson was sentenced to transportation for fifteen years after he was found guilty of a highway robbery in Manchester. The victim was a wealthy brewer named Jonathan Andrew who resided at Hendham Hall, Harpurhey.

Manchester Market Place, *c.*1900.

At half past nine on the evening of 3 October, Andrew was walking home along St George's Road when he was violently assaulted by three men. The men knocked him to the ground, leaving him unconscious, and stole three £10 bank notes and seven sovereigns.

The following day, Wilson went to a hatter's shop in the Market Place and purchased a hat with one of the stolen bank notes. He was later apprehended and a bloodstained shirt was found in his pocket. After hearing the evidence, the jury found him guilty of the highway robbery and sentenced him to fifteen years' transportation.

On 13 March 1844, Wilson set sail on board a ship called *Blundell* for Van Diemen's Land (now known as Tasmania). The treacherous passage took eight months and the ship arrived on 13 November 1844. There was no evidence to suggest that he ever came back to England.

20 DECEMBER 1899 The inquest resumed into the poisoning of two male inmates at the Crumpsall Workhouse Hospital. The victims were 65-year-old William Wharton and 60-year-old John Smith.

A nurse named Sarah Gibson stated that on the previous Thursday she had given Smith two tablespoons of medicine from a bottle that had his name on it. Shortly after taking the medicine, Smith began complaining that he felt unwell and was struggling to breathe. Wharton had also received some medicine that had been made at the same time as Smith's. Both gentlemen later died as a result of taking the medicine.

It was revealed at the inquest that the medicine was made at the hospital dispensary, and whoever had made the solution had mistakenly added the poison strychnine – a grain of this poison was enough to cause death. The mistake was the fault of the chief dispenser and his two assistants, but none of them admitted to making up the medicine.

Summing up, the judge ordered that all poisons should be kept under lock and key, and kept in different shaped bottles to avoid this happening again in the future.

21 DECEMBER 1870 This week, the body of a 15-year-old girl named Charlotte Knight was found in the Ashton Canal between Mill Street and Pollard Street. Charlotte had been missing since 10 December. On the night she went missing, she had been arguing with her father, who had reprimanded her for taking her time to run an errand and for using foul language. The father then summoned her to clean the scullery and that was the last time she was seen alive.

22 DECEMBER 1855 An inquest was held into the mysterious poisoning of a maid named Elizabeth Cooper, who was in the service of a Manchester surgeon named John Moss Kirkham.

The incident had begun on the previous Tuesday after Elizabeth had been accused of stealing by one of the other members of staff. Elizabeth protested her innocence and got into a heated argument with one of the other maids, at which point Mrs Kirkham intervened and told Elizabeth that she was dismissed.

The following day, Mrs Kirkham went and fetched Elizabeth's sister Martha. When the pair arrived at the Kirkhams' residence, they went to the maid's room and found her leaning over a washbowl vomiting violently. Martha attempted to get her home, although it was evident that she was very sick.

Once home, Martha and her father nursed the ill girl throughout the night. The next morning her condition had deteriorated further and the doctor was called. By the time he arrived, however, the girl had passed away.

At the inquest it was revealed that Elizabeth had died as a result of being poisoned. Members of the Kirkham household were questioned and they revealed that the maid had a violent temper and possibly administered the poison herself. However, Martha was convinced that her sister had been deliberately poisoned after she complained to another maid about the conduct of Mr Kirkham who, Martha claimed, had abused her sister and had threatened her after he heard that she had spoken to another maid. He denied all the claims.

The jury at the inquest ruled that Elizabeth Cooper had been poisoned but they did not have sufficient evidence to say who had administered it.

23 DECEMBER 1881 On this day, a sailor named Alfred Walton appeared at the City Police Court charged with throwing acid in the face of Amy Harris. It appeared that some time previous, the couple had been courting, but after a series of arguments, Miss Harris had ended their relationship.

On the previous Wednesday morning, Amy had been walking down Rochdale Road when she bumped into Walton at the corner of Pump Street. He asked her if her feelings were the same as they were a few weeks previous when she ended their courtship, to which Amy replied that her feelings were unchanged. In a desperate bid to rekindle the relationship, he asked to meet her later on that evening, but she declined. Walton then told Amy that there was something on her face. He then calmly placed his hand in his pocket, pulled out a cloth and began to wipe her face. Immediately her face began to burn – the cloth was soaked in vitriol. Walton offered no help; instead he stood there laughing. With the acid burning the skin off her face, Amy managed to stagger into a chemist's shop to get assistance. Walton fled the scene. Amy Harris survived the attack but was left with a permanent scar on the left side of her face from her eye to her jaw.

Alfred Walton was found guilty at the City Police Court and sent for trial at the assizes on 28 January 1882. He admitted his guilt and was sentenced to eighteen months in prison with hard labour.

24 DECEMBER 1852 Tragedy occurred this week in the district of Hulme when a newborn child was discovered in an ash pit. The child was found alive in the pit in Scott Street, but died the following Wednesday in the workhouse on Stretford Road. The inquest revealed that the child had been murdered by strangulation. The mother of the child – and the murderer – were never found.

25 DECEMBER 1898 A tram inspector named Samuel Brown died after being stabbed on Oxford Street two days previous.

On Friday evening, Brown had been out drinking when he got into a quarrel with an American man named John George Turner. After some words were exchanged, Turner propositioned Brown to a fight. Brown hit first and knocked Turner to the floor. Turner then got up and stabbed Brown on the left side of his chest with a dagger. The injured man was taken to the Manchester Royal Infirmary and then to the Salford Royal Hospital, where he died two days later.

Turner was later arrested and charged with wilful murder. On 1 February 1899, he was sentenced at the Manchester Assizes to death by hanging. Two weeks later, the Home Secretary commuted the sentence to penal servitude for life.

26 DECEMBER 1910 The *Manchester Guardian* reported on the tragic death of 19-year-old Edward D'Andrade from Portugal. During the previous twelve months he had fallen in love with a girl who lived on Cecil Street. However, the parents of the girl objected to their relationship and refused to allow their daughter to enter into an engagement with the young man. The family also banned the young man from ever entering their home again.

On Christmas Day, D'Andrade turned up at his lover's home and handed her a bundle of letters that she had written to him. Confused by his actions, she invited him in and the pair entered the front room. As she went to light the gas, Edward bent down and kissed her softly on the cheek. In the darkness, the heartbroken man put a gun to his head and pulled the trigger. He died instantly.

27 DECEMBER 1902 An inquest was held on the body of 28-year-old George Harwood, who died on Christmas Day. Harwood left his house early that morning to play a football match. He was the captain of the North Manchester Football Club and on that day they were playing the Broughton Hornets at Whalley Range.

At the end of the game, neither side had scored, so it was decided to play ten minutes each way extra time. The final whistle of extra time was about to be blown when two Hornet midfielders made an attack down the centre of the pitch. Harwood ran over and attempted a tackle, which brought all three players crashing to the ground. The two Hornet players got up immediately, but Harwood lay lifeless on the ground. Several men ran over to help but he was out cold. He was transferred to the Manchester Infirmary but unfortunately died at half past nine that evening, having never regained consciousness.

28 DECEMBER 1915 Fred Holmes was committed for trial at the assizes for the murder of 38-year-old Sarah Woodall. The crime took place sometime between 6 and 7 December at a lodging house on Clifford Street – which was situated in the district of Oxford Road.

On the morning of 7 December, Holmes left the house and did not return. The landlady went to check his bedroom and found that the door had been blocked. After forcing her way inside, she made the gruesome discovery of a woman's body. Holmes was arrested the following day.

At his trial it was revealed that the couple were in a relationship. Some time in the early hours of the morning they had an argument and in a rage, Holmes attacked Sarah, cutting her throat with a razor and killing her almost immediately. Holmes then barricaded the door, which gave him enough time to escape through a window.

It took the jury fifty minutes to find Holmes guilty of the murder of Sarah Woodall. He was sentenced to death. His execution took place at Strangeways prison on 8 March 1916.

29 DECEMBER 1876 Mary Walker (alias Ann Kelly) was in prison on this day after being sentenced to three months for being a thief. Between 1876 and 1883, Walker received three convictions for being a rogue and a vagabond, and six convictions for larceny. She committed crimes in Yorkshire and Manchester.

Manchester thief Mary Walker, alias Ann Kelly.

30 DECEMBER 1836 This week, a group of young thieves were operating in the district of Deansgate. Their targets were goods that were on display in shop windows and doors.

On the previous Wednesday, a prolific 14-year-old thief named George Donaldson was walking past Hooper's draper shop when he spotted a piece of flannel on display in the door. While the shopkeeper was distracted, he grabbed the cloth and fled. A passer-by witnessed the theft and gave chase, eventually catching the lad in the cellar of a house on Watson Street. The flannel was eventually found concealed under a bed.

Donaldson was apprehended and sent for trial. On 9 January 1837, he was found guilty and sentenced to seven years' transportation. On 9 February he was transferred from prison to the hulk ship *Euryalus*, which was docked at Chatham. Sometime between 24 and 29 August, he was loaded – along with another 148 convicts – on board the *Royal Sovereign* and his passage to Tasmania began. Donaldson was now 15 years old. The voyage took eight months and the ship finally arrived in Van Diemen's Land on 29 April 1838.

31 DECEMBER 1857 A respectable-looking man named Charles Browness was spending his first New Year's Eve in prison. The gentleman was awaiting trial for stealing the pocketbook of Frederick Thompson from a table in the Corn Exchange. But this was no ordinary theft: the book contained £3,111.

On 10 December, Thompson – who was a partner in a millers' firm in Wakefield – was in Manchester to conduct some business in the Corn Exchange. The Exchange was particularly busy on that day, with swarms of traders bartering to get the best deal. Thompson arrived there at half past eleven in the morning. Shortly after one o'clock in the afternoon, he placed his book on the table. At around half past one, he noticed the book was missing and initially blamed a man named Mr Radford who, he assumed, had taken it for a joke.

When the money was not found, the police were summoned and a hunt for the thief began. Suspicion soon fell on a 'foreign' man who was wearing an Oxford grey overcoat and a cravat that was fastened with an elegant pin.

A police officer and a man from the Corn Exchange named Thorpe took a cab to the train station, with the intention of stopping the thief if he tried to board a train. The stationmaster stated that a man fitting the description of the 'foreign' man was already on board a train heading from Victoria Station to Liverpool. The two men joined the train and found the gentleman sat with two ladies in one of the carriages. The officer attempted to ask the man if he was heading for Liverpool, but the man replied in broken English that he did not understand because 'he was a foreigner'. The officer explained that he would need to leave the train with him at the next station. As the men got off at the next station, a struggle took place and the officer placed his hand in the man's top pocket and pulled out a bundle of notes. The officer then charged the man with robbing Thompson at the Corn Exchange. The man then confessed to his crime and revealed that his name was Charles Browness.

Browness was brought up at the Borough Court on 11 December, where the evidence was heard and he was sent for trial at the next city sessions. The trial began on 5 January 1858 before R.B. Armstrong QC. Representing the prisoner was a man named Mr Wheeler. The recorder stated that he had no doubt that the man had travelled from Liverpool to Manchester with the intention to steal; however, he did acknowledge that Browness could not have known how much he had taken at the time of the robbery, and so he was sentenced to one year's hard labour. Browness stood perfectly still with his eyes closed and his hands by his side throughout the proceedings. He showed no emotion as the sentence was passed.

BIBLIOGRAPHY

Books

Briggs, A., *Victorian Cities* (London: Penguin, 1990)

Engels, F., *The Condition of the Working-Class in England in 1844* (London: George Allen & Unwin, 1943)

Hylton, S., *A History of Manchester* (Chichester: Phillimore, 2003)

Marlow, J., *The Peterloo Massacre* (London: Granada Publishing Ltd, 1971)

Messinger, G.S., *Manchester in the Victorian Age* (Manchester: Manchester University Press, 1985)

Storey, N.R., *The Victorian Criminal* (Oxford: Shire Library, 2011)

Websites

www.ancestry.co.uk

www.burialrecords.manchester.gov.uk

www.executedtoday.com

www.findmypast.co.uk

www.lancastercastle.com

www.proquest.com

Other

Court Leet Records 1552–1686 (Manchester: Henry Blacklock & Co., 1888)

Court Leet Records 1731–1846 (Manchester: Henry Blacklock & Co., 1888)

England & Wales, Criminal Registers, 1791–1892 (www.ancestry.co.uk)

Manchester Prison Registers 1847–1881 (www.findmypast.co.uk)

Prison Ship (Hulk) Registers 1811–1843 (findmypast.co.uk)

Manchester Courier and Lancashire General Advertiser (1825–1916)

Manchester Mercury (1759–1826)

Manchester Times (1828–1900)

Manchester Guardian (1821–1950)

Manchester Historical Recorder, 1874
The Thieves Book (Greater Manchester Police Museum)

List of Illustrations

Visit our website and discover thousands of other History Press books.

www.thehistorypress.co.uk